Paula Wagner   Nice Productions   LPO
New Regency Productions
Caiola Productions & Co.   James L. Nederlander   Roy Furman   Hun
Graham Burke   Edward Walson   deRoy Kierstead   Michael Cass
Stage Entertainment   Ambassador Theatre Group   The John Gore O
EXECUTIVE PRODUCERS
Wendy Orshan and Jeffrey M. Wilson

PRETTY THE MUSICAL WOMAN

BOOK BY
Garry Marshall & J.F. Lawton

MUSIC AND LYRICS BY
Bryan Adams & Jim Vallance

Based on the Touchstone Pictures motion picture written by J.F. Lawton

STARRING

Samantha Barks AND Steve Kazee

WITH

Eric Anderson   Jason Danieley   Kingsley Leggs

Allison Blackwell   Tommy Bracco   Brian Cali   Robby Clater
Jessica Crouch   Anna Eilinsfeld   Matt Farcher   Lauren Lim Jackson
Renée Marino   Ellyn Marie Marsh   Jake Odmark   Jillian Mueller   Jennifer Sanchez
Matthew Stocke   Alex Michael Stoll   Alan Wiggins   Jesse Wildman   Darius Wright

AND

Orfeh

SCENIC DESIGN	COSTUME DESIGN	LIGHTING DESIGN	SOUND DESIGN
David Rockwell	**Gregg Barnes**	**Kenneth Posner** **Philip S. Rosenberg**	**John Shivers**

HAIR DESIGN	PUPPET DESIGN	MAKEUP DESIGN	ASSOCIATE DIRECTOR	ASSOCIATE CHOREOGRAPHER
Josh Marquette	**James Ortiz**	**Fiona Mifsud**	**DB Bonds**	**Rusty Mowery**

CASTING	TECHNICAL SUPERVISOR	PRODUCTION STAGE MANAGER	MUSIC COORDINATOR	COMPANY MANAGER
Telsey + Company **Craig Burns, CSA**	**Theatersmith** **Associates, LLC**	**Thomas Recktenwald**	**Michael Keller** **Michael Aarons**	**Rina L. Saltzman**

ADVERTISING & MARKETING	DIGITAL MARKETING	PRESS REPRESENTATIVE	ASSOCIATE PRODUCER	GENERAL MANAGER
SpotCo	**Situation Interactive**	**Polk & Co.**	**Sara Bottfeld**	**101 Productions, Ltd.**

MUSIC SUPERVISION, ARRANGEMENTS AND ORCHESTRATIONS BY
Will Van Dyke

DIRECTED AND CHOREOGRAPHED BY
Jerry Mitchell

ISBN: 978-1-5400-4209-5

7777 W. BLUEMOUND RD. P.O. BOX 13819 MILWAUKEE, WI 53213

Visit Hal Leonard Online at
www.halleonard.com

Contact us:
Hal Leonard
7777 West Bluemound Road
Milwaukee, WI 53213
Email: info@halleonard.com

In Europe, contact:
Hal Leonard Europe Limited
42 Wigmore Street
Marylebone, London, W1U 2RN
Email: info@halleonardeurope.com

In Australia, contact:
Hal Leonard Australia Pty. Ltd.
4 Lentara Court
Cheltenham, Victoria, 3192 Australia
Email: info@halleonard.com.au

WELCOME TO HOLLYWOOD

Words and Music by BRYAN ADAMS
and JIM VALLANCE

map to your life— you'll be lost ___ un - til you've caught ___ one.

Look at her— she's ___ got dreams of ___ her

own deep ___ in - side. How do I know? It's my job, ___ I'm your guide. ___ So

stick with me ___ and you'll see ___ where this is go - ing.

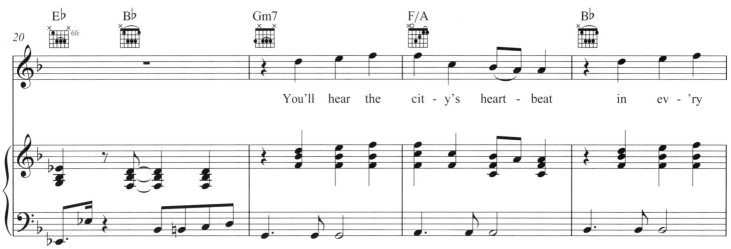

You'll hear the cit-y's heart-beat in ev-'ry

square of con-crete.__ Come fol-low me now— Wel-come to Hol-ly-wood!__

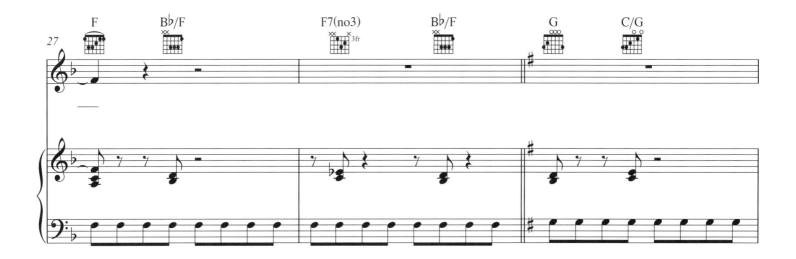

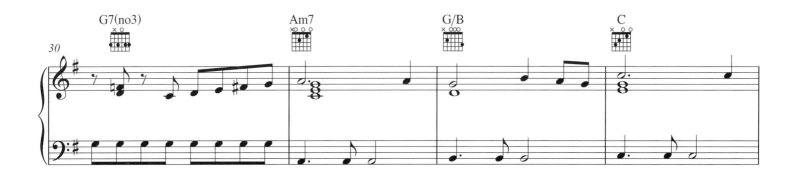

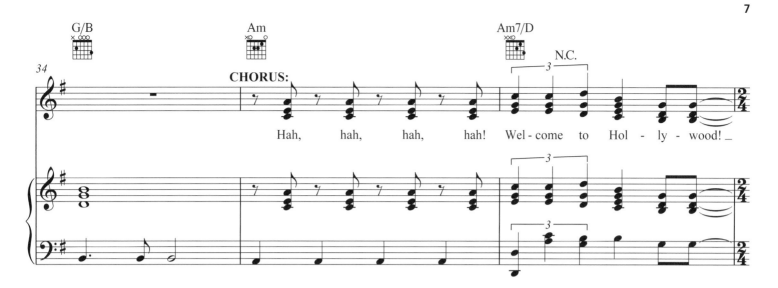

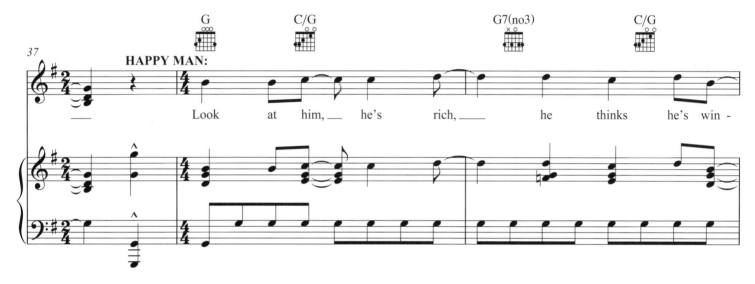

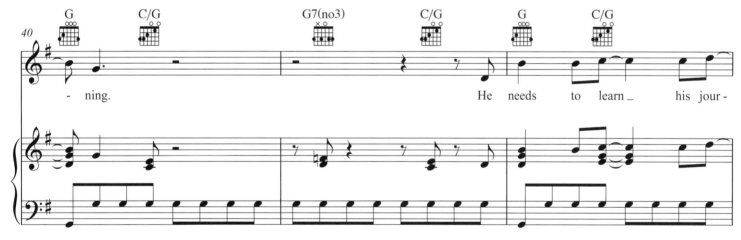

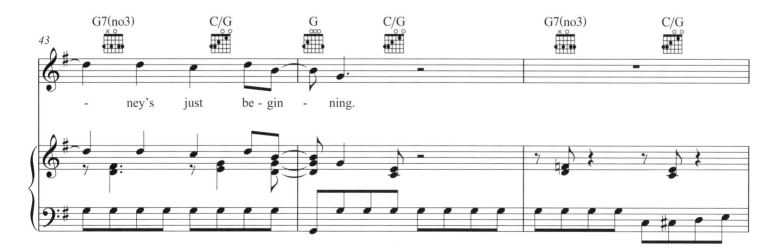

8

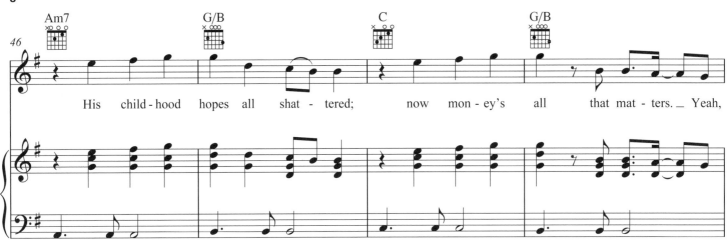

His child-hood hopes all shat-tered; now mon-ey's all that mat-ters. __ Yeah,

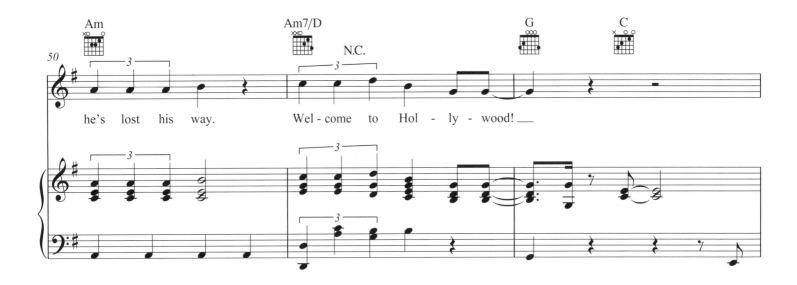

he's lost his way. Wel - come to Hol - ly - wood! __

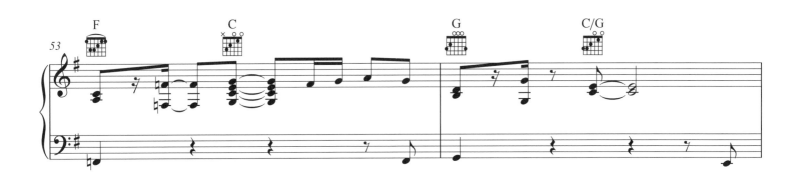

HAPPY MAN:

There's dan - ger on __ the street; __ it's all a - round __

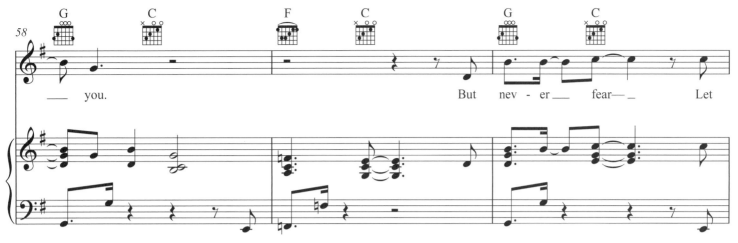

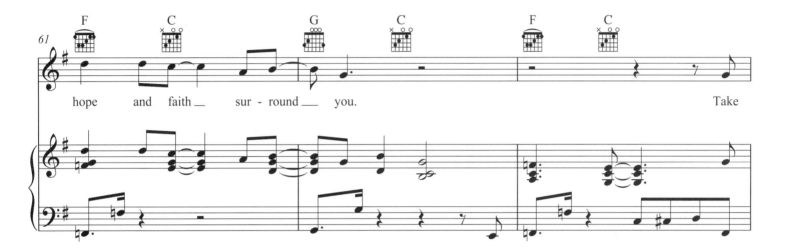

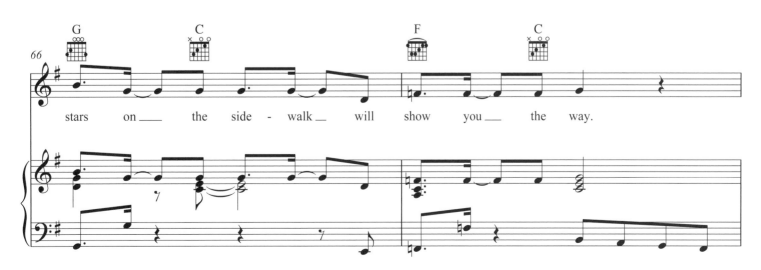

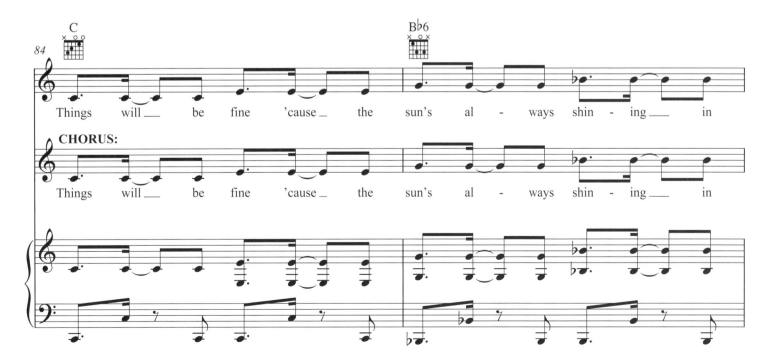

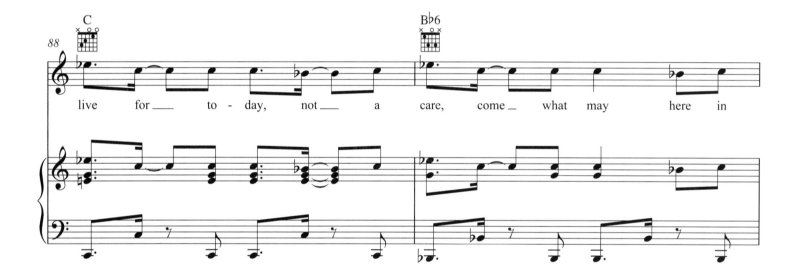

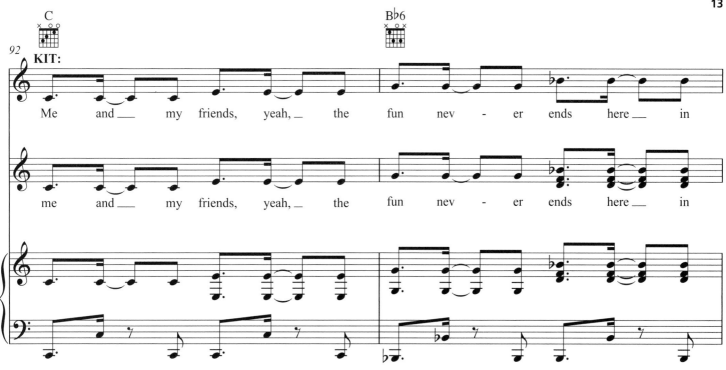

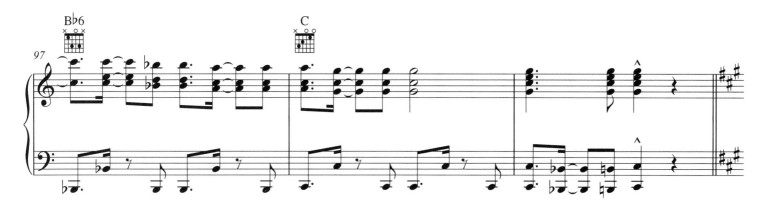

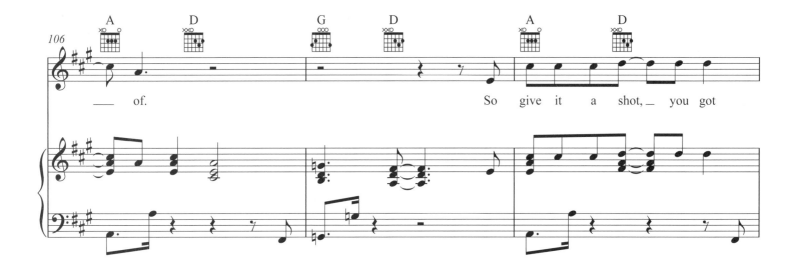

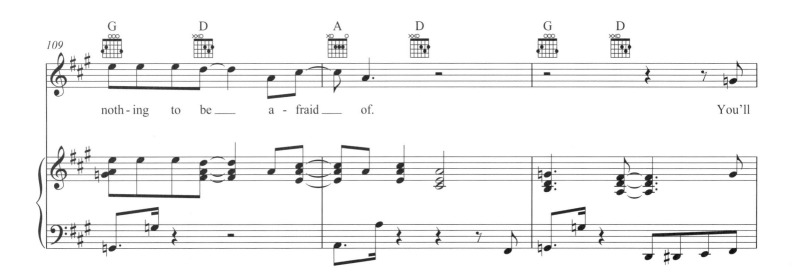

see me ___ here, ___ and you'll see me ___ there. ___ You

CHORUS:

We've all got

just might see me ev - 'ry - where, _ but first you must _ be - lieve. _

hopes and dreams, but first you must _ be - lieve. _

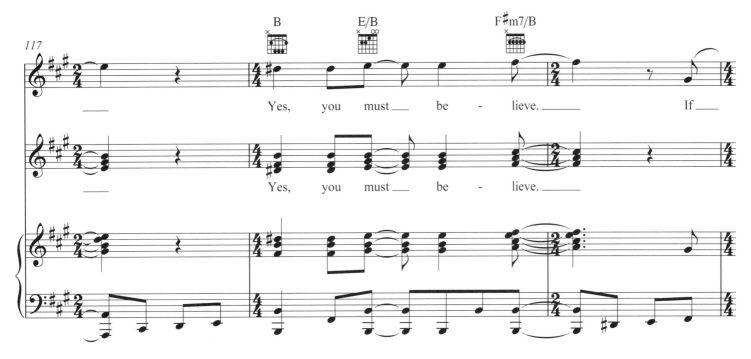

___ Yes, you must ___ be - lieve. ___ If ___

Yes, you must ___ be - lieve. ___

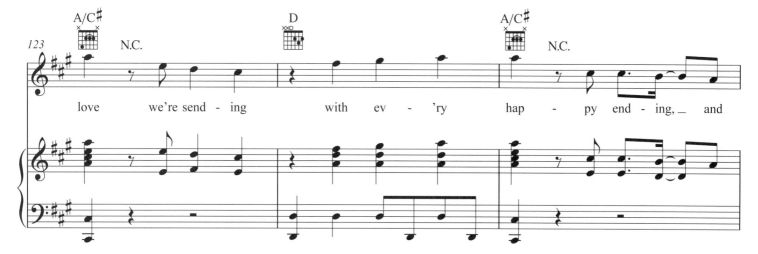

ANYWHERE BUT HERE

Words and Music by BRYAN ADAMS
and JIM VALLANCE

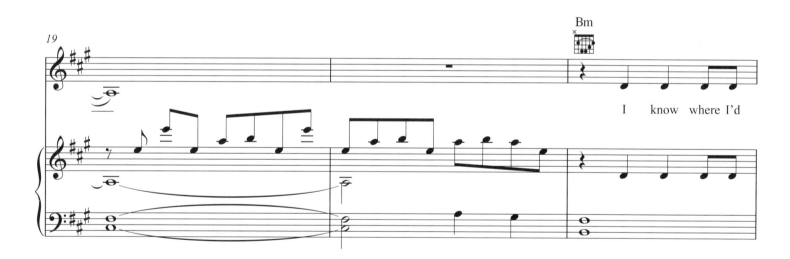

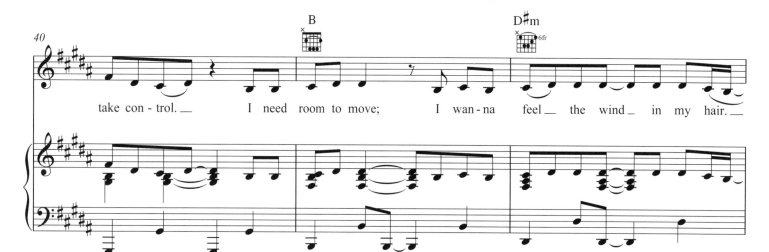

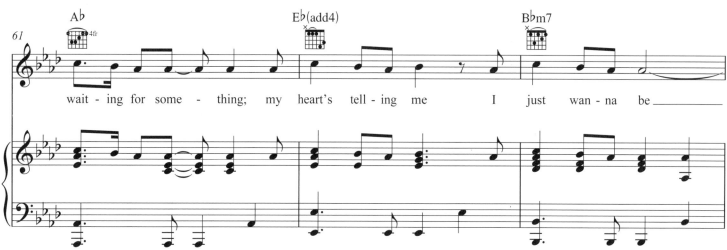

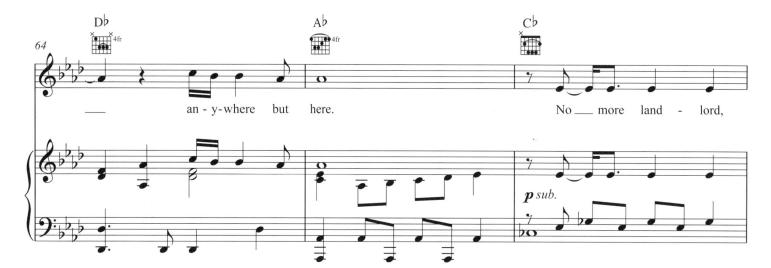

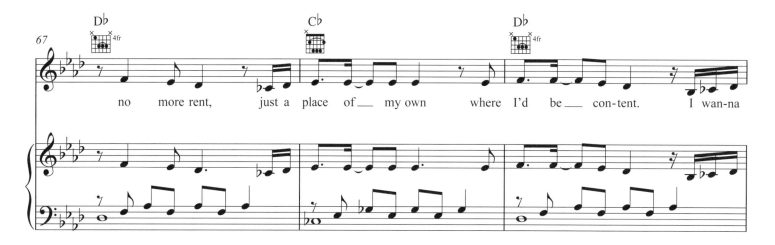

I be-lieve some-how, __ some - day, __ that's the way it __ will

Take it home!

be, an-y-where but here, _____ an-y-where but

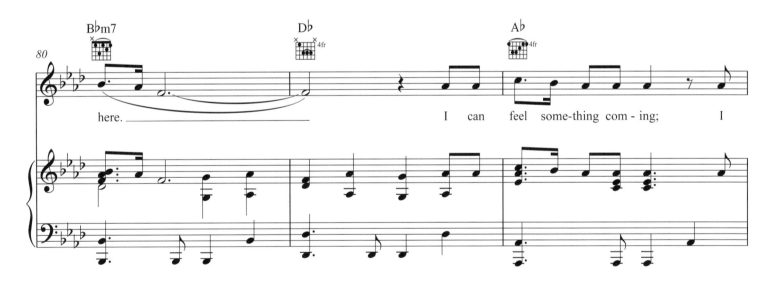

here. _____ I can feel some-thing com - ing; I

long to be free. __ I just wan - na be _____ an - y - where, __

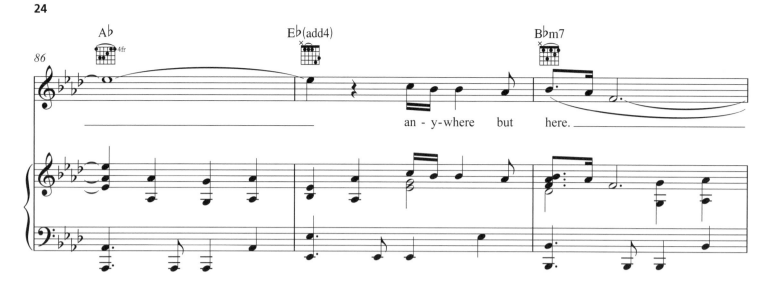

an-y-where but here.

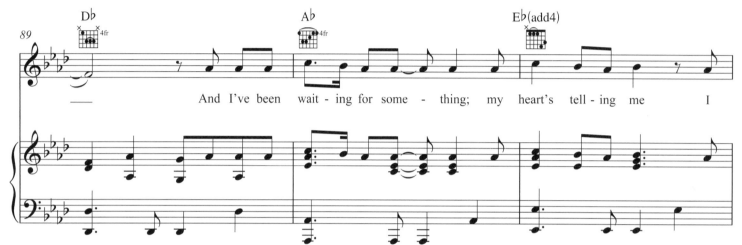

And I've been wait-ing for some - thing; my heart's tell-ing me I

just wan - na be _____ an-y-where but here. _____

SOMETHING ABOUT HER

Words and Music by BRYAN ADAMS
and JIM VALLANCE

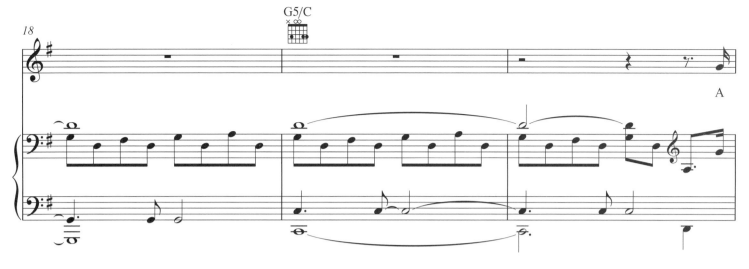

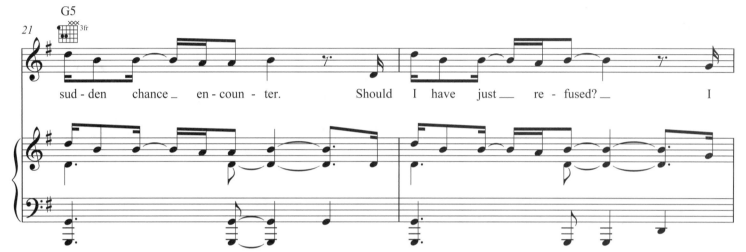

sud - den chance __ en - coun - ter. Should I have just __ re - fused? __ I

asked her for __ di - rec - tions; now I feel __ con - fused. __ I can't

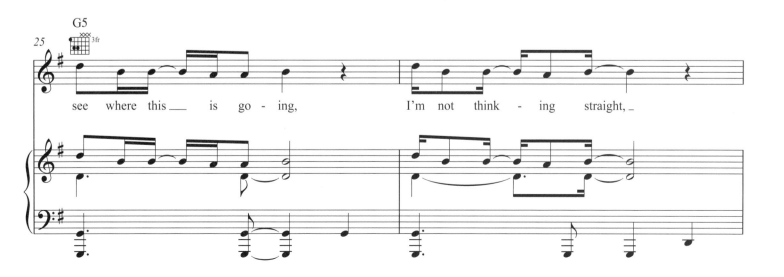

see where this __ is go - ing, I'm not think - ing straight, __

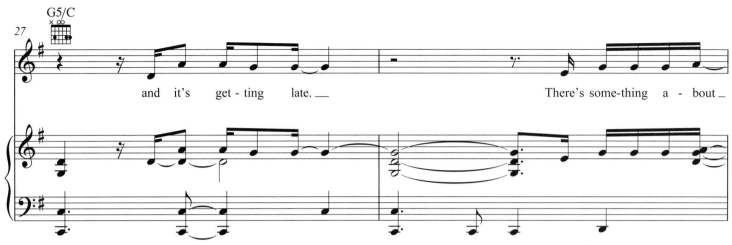

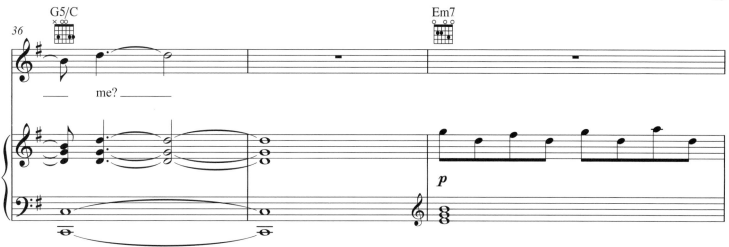

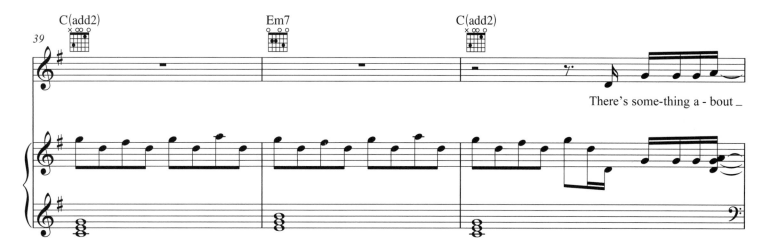

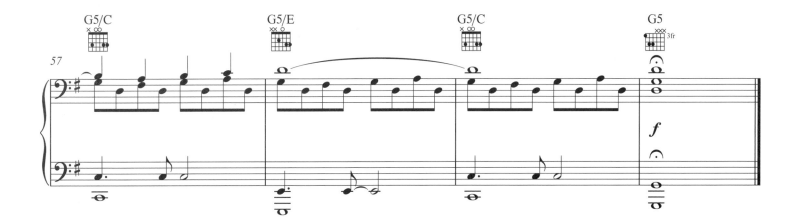

LUCKIEST GIRL IN THE WORLD

Words and Music by BRYAN ADAMS
and JIM VALLANCE

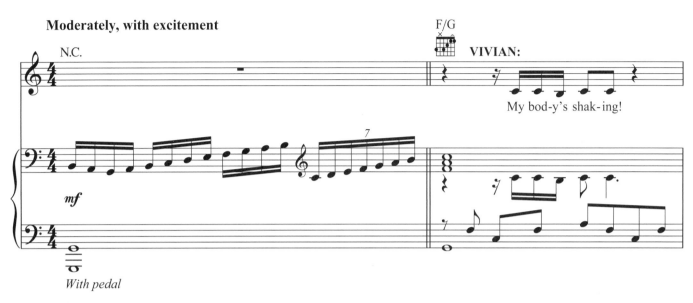

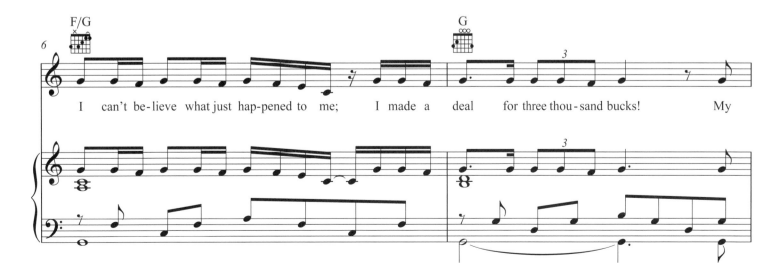

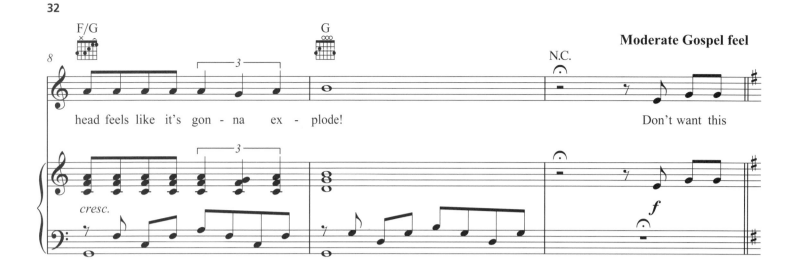

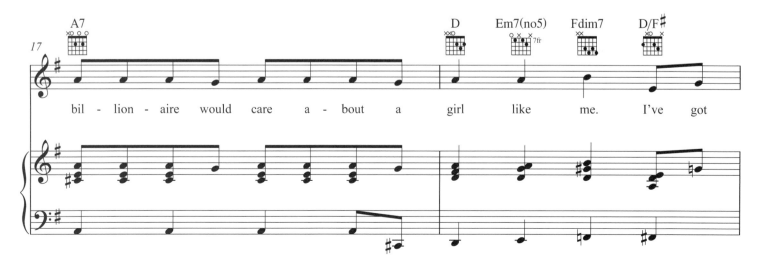

mon-ey to spend; _ I've got cham-pagne on ice. _ There's a smile on my face; _ I'm get-ting

treat-ed real _ nice. I'm start-ing to feel _ like the luck-i-est girl _ in the

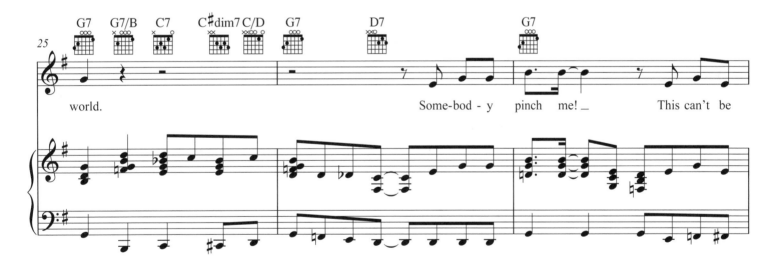

world. Some-bod-y pinch me! _ This can't be

true. If I de-serve this, tell me what did I _ do? He _ could

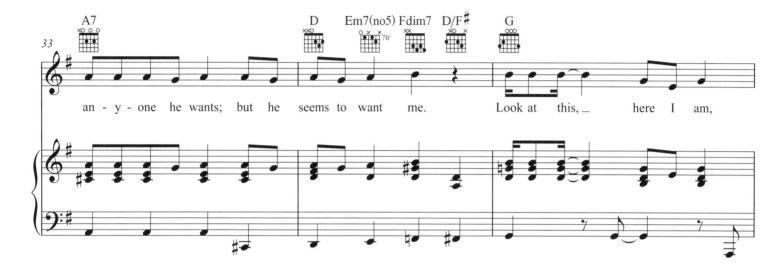

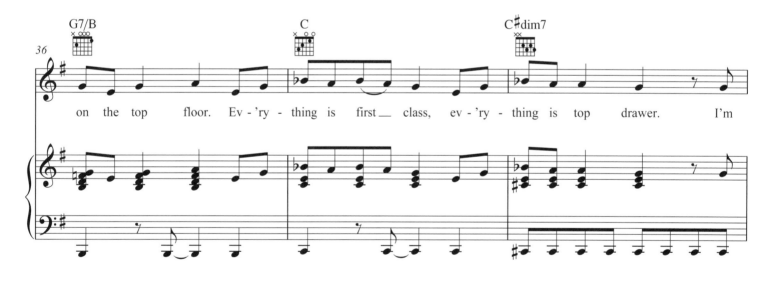

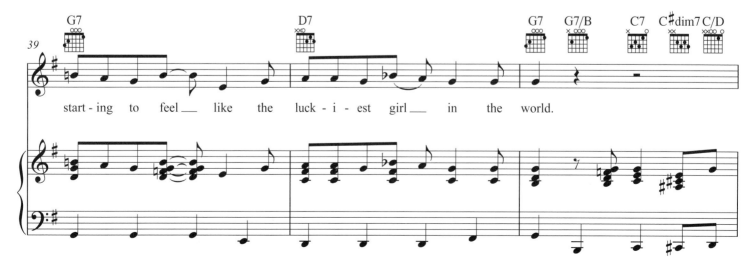

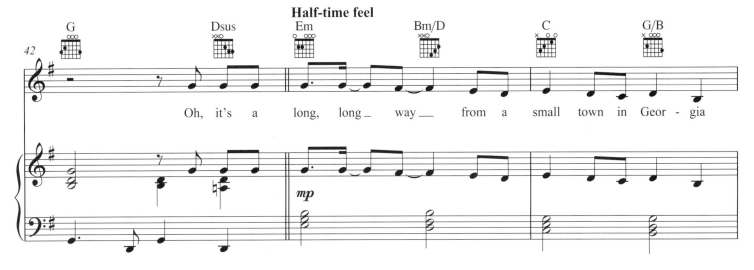

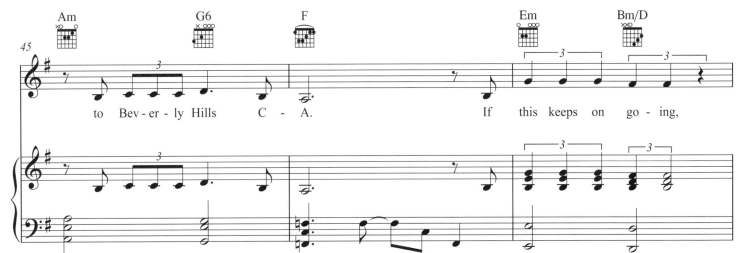

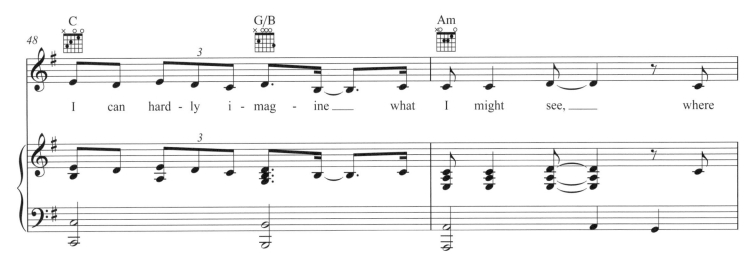

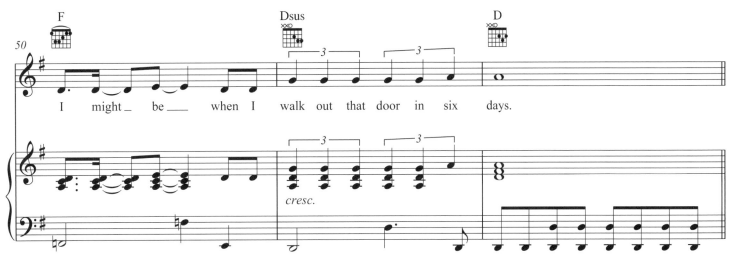

RODEO DRIVE

Words and Music by BRYAN ADAMS
and JIM VALLANCE

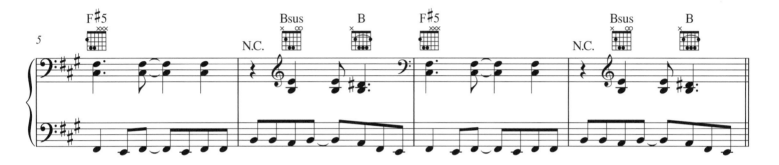

we're gon - na make his day. ____ So start to make your

way to _____ Ro - de - o Drive, ba - by. Yeah, _

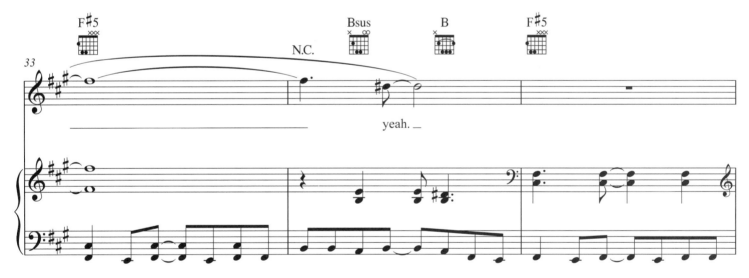

_____ yeah. _

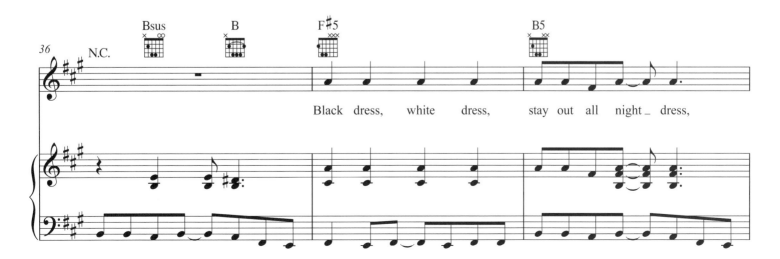

Black dress, white dress, stay out all night _ dress,

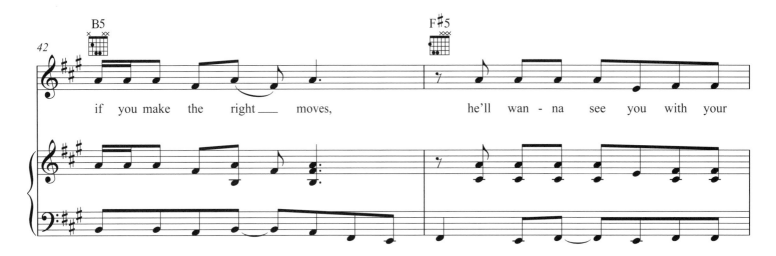

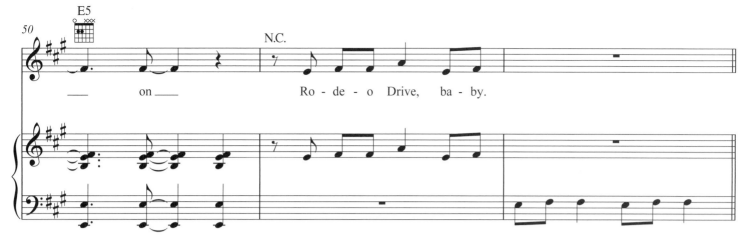

on __ Ro - de - o Drive, ba - by.

Half-time feel

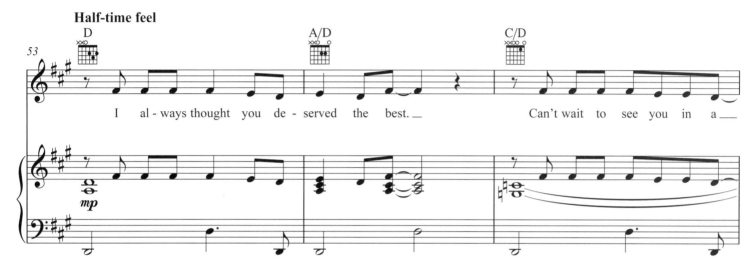

I al - ways thought you de - served the best. __ Can't wait to see you in a __

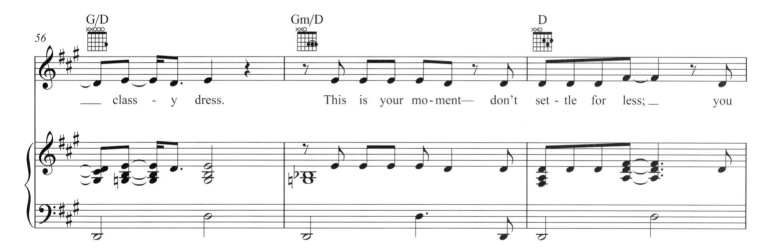

__ class - y dress. This is your mo - ment— don't set - tle for less; __ you

know you can't __ go wrong. __ You don't be - long __ on the __

ON A NIGHT LIKE TONIGHT

Words and Music by BRYAN ADAMS
and JIM VALLANCE

Moderate Latin groove, with romantic flair

MR. THOMPSON:

On a night like to-night, just re-mem-ber you're right where you're meant to be. In a daz-zl-ing dress, __ I'm sure you'll im-press; __ this I guar-an-tee.

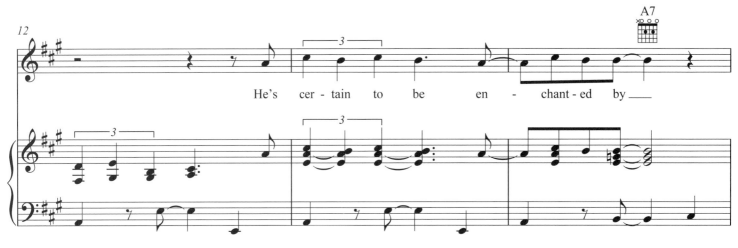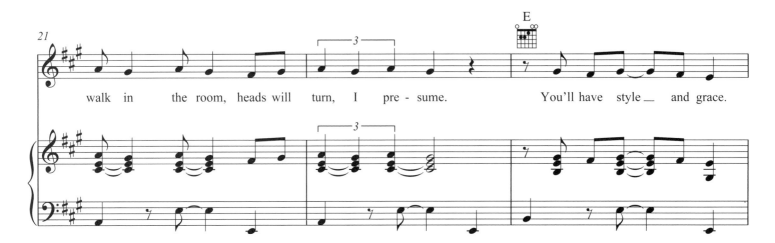

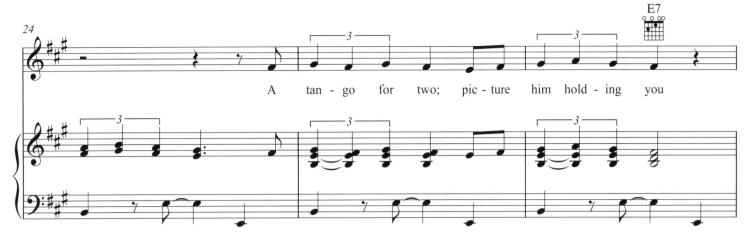

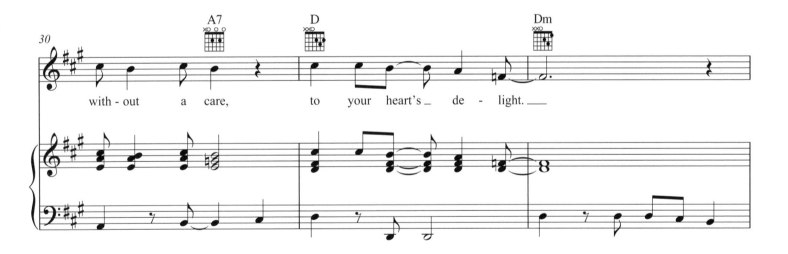

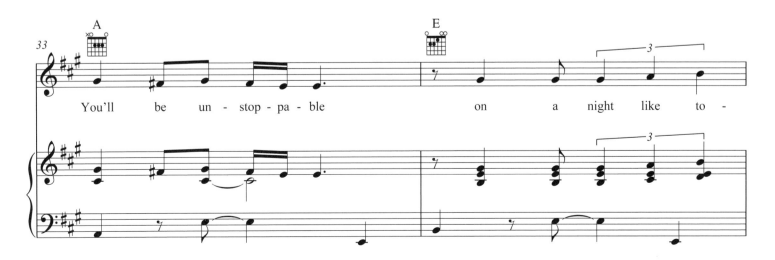

night. Now, re-mem-ber, be true to your-

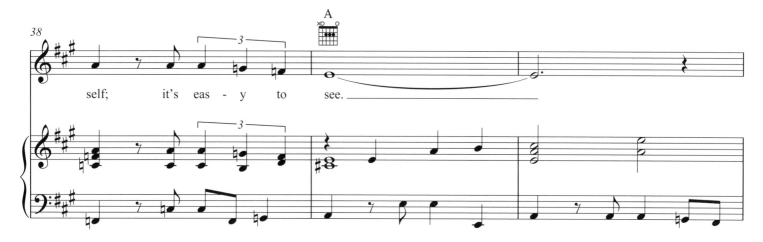

self; it's eas-y to see. _____

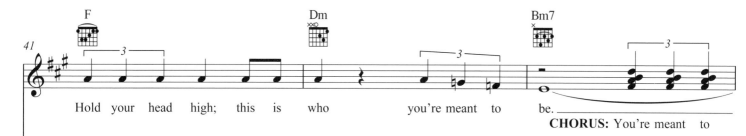

Hold your head high; this is who you're meant to be. _____

CHORUS: You're meant to

be. When you walk in the room, heads will turn, I pre-sume.
When you walk in the room.

You'll have style __ and grace.　　　A tan - go for two; pic - ture
CHORUS: A tan - go for

him hold - ing you　　　in a warm em - brace.
two.

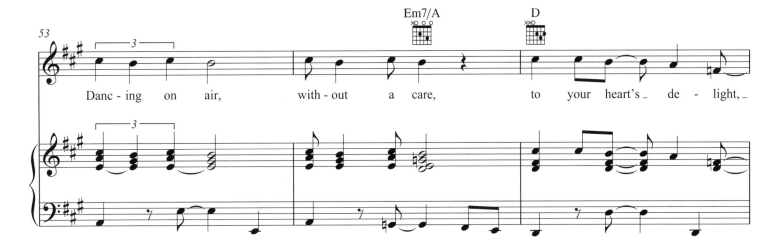

Danc - ing on air,　with - out a care,　to your heart's __ de - light, __

__ you'll be un - stop - pa - ble　on a night like to -

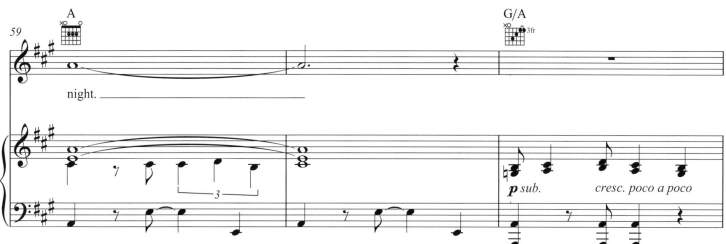

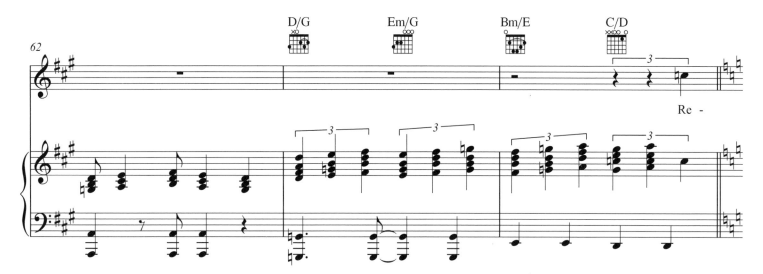

night.

Re-mem - ber, be true to your - self; it's eas - y to see.

Hold your head high; this is who you're meant to

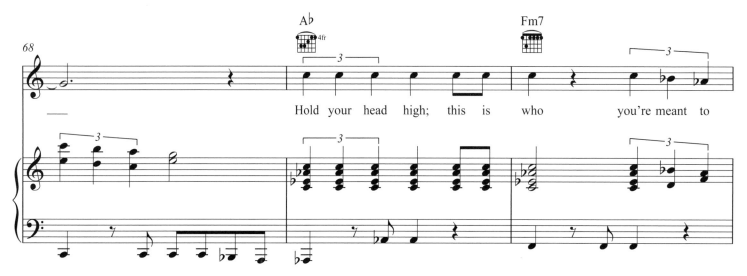

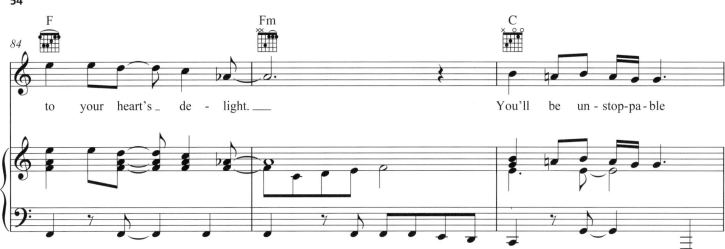

to your heart's _ de - light. ___ You'll be un - stop - pa - ble

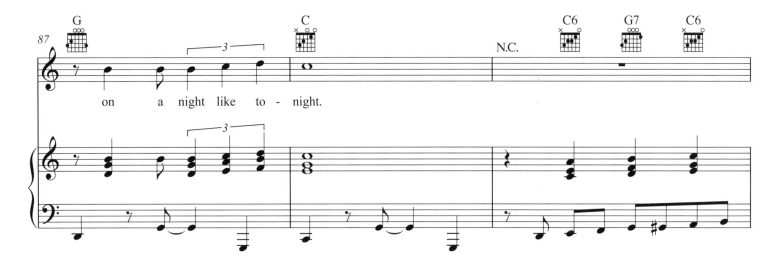

on a night like to - night.

An - y - thing's pos - si - ble on a night like to - night, _____

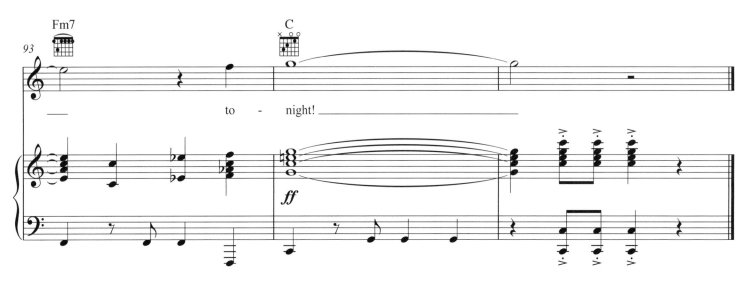

to - night! _____

DON'T FORGET TO DANCE

Words and Music by BRYAN ADAMS
and JIM VALLANCE

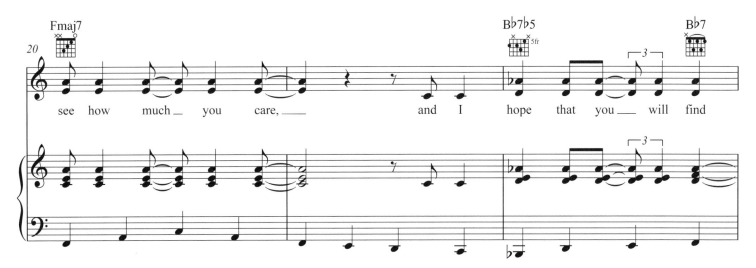

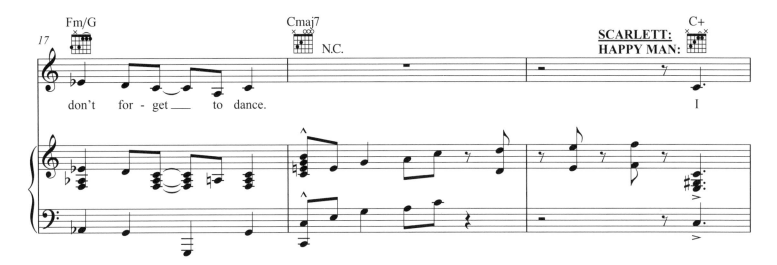

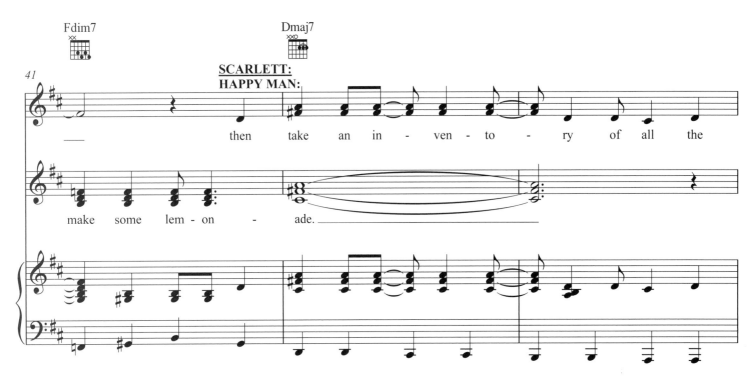

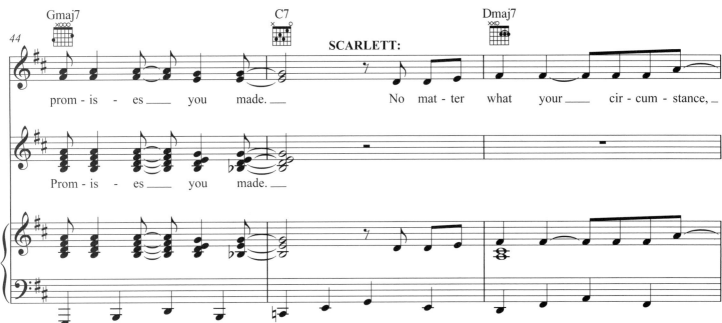

FREEDOM

Words and Music by BRYAN ADAMS
and JIM VALLANCE

Calmly, unhurried

What a strange night; and yet it feels right.

How was I to know she would show me

who I could real-ly be? I can't keep hold-ing on; I've

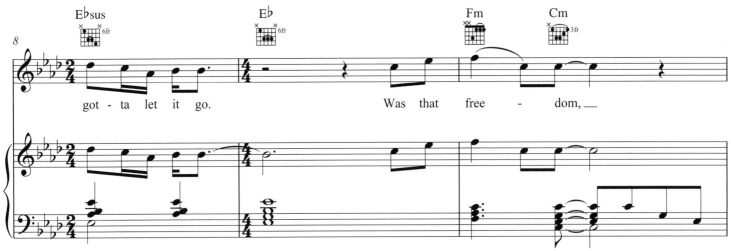

got-ta let it go. Was that free - dom, ___

free - dom, ___ when we were danc - ing ___ on the floor? ___

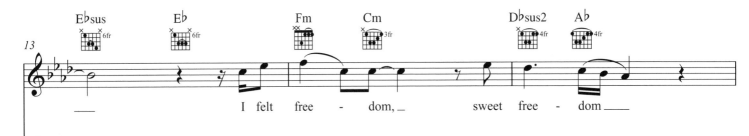

___ I felt free - dom, ___ sweet free - dom ___

like I've nev-er felt ___ be-fore; ___ and I know that I need ___

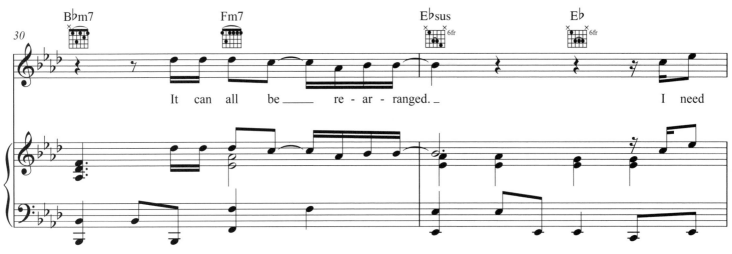

It can all be ___ re - ar - ranged. ___ I need

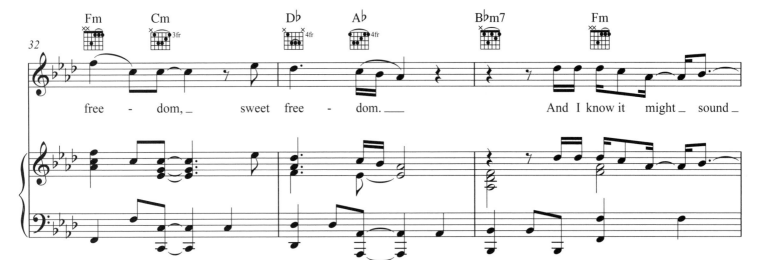

free - dom, ___ sweet free - dom. ___ And I know it might ___ sound ___

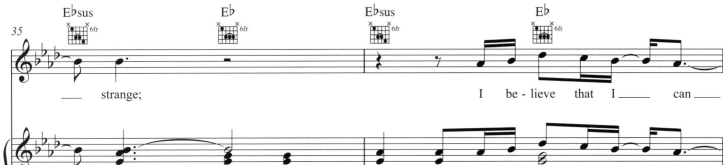

___ strange; I be - lieve that I ___ can ___

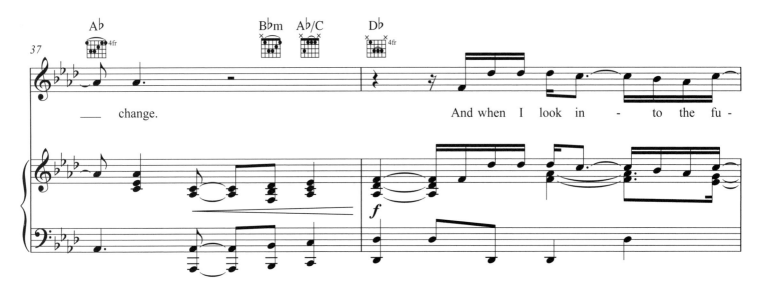

___ change. And when I look in - to the fu -

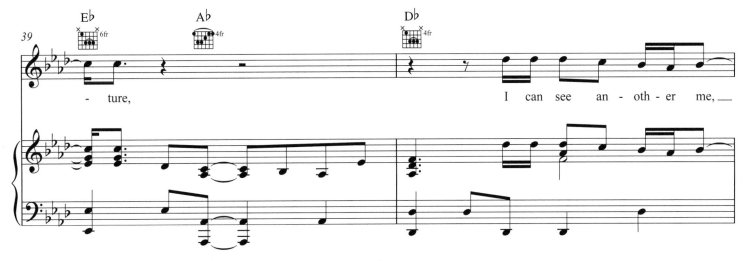

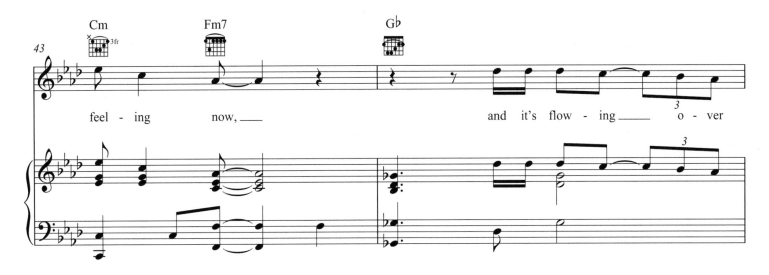

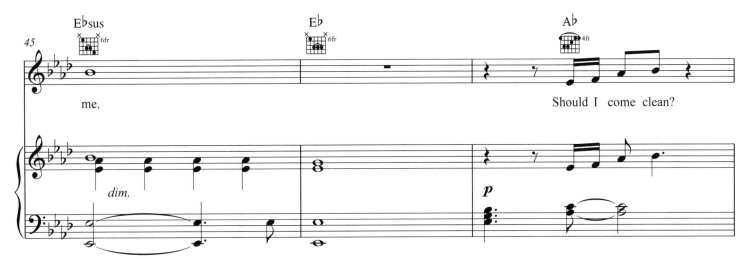

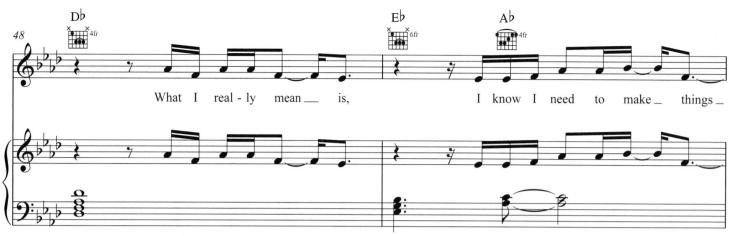

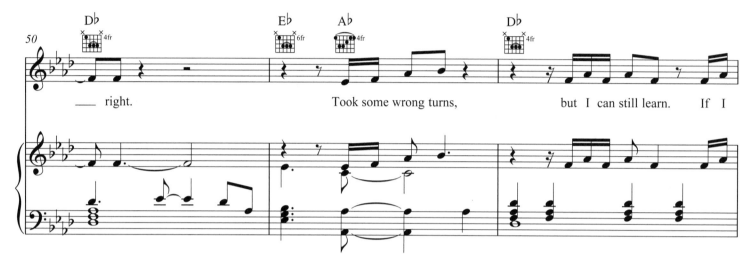

YOU'RE BEAUTIFUL

Words and Music by BRYAN ADAMS
and JIM VALLANCE

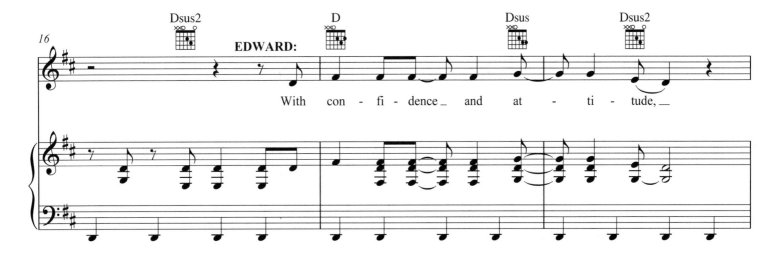

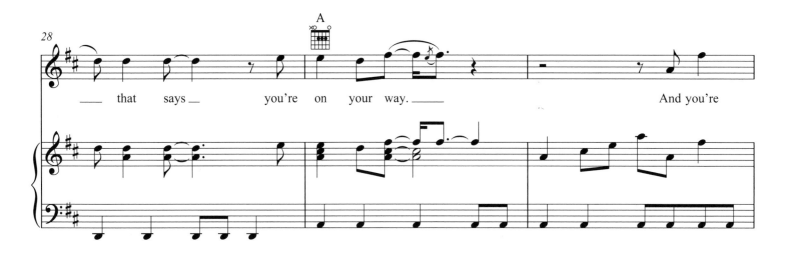

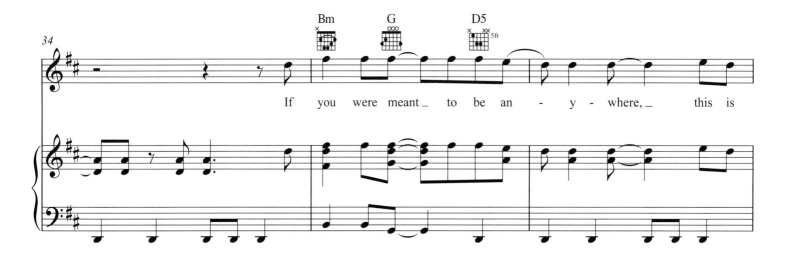

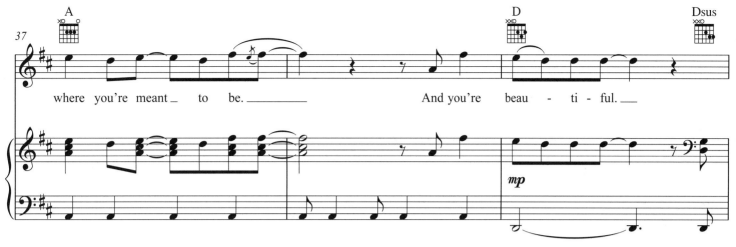

where you're meant _ to be. _____ And you're beau - ti - ful. _

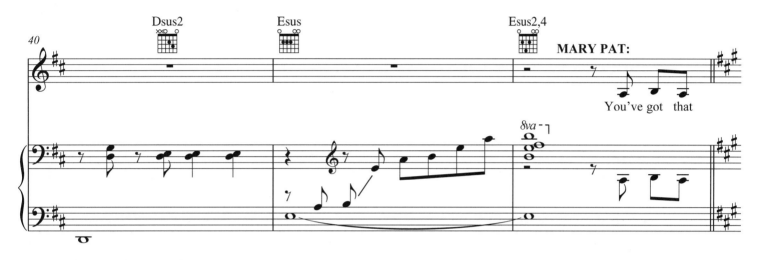

You've got that

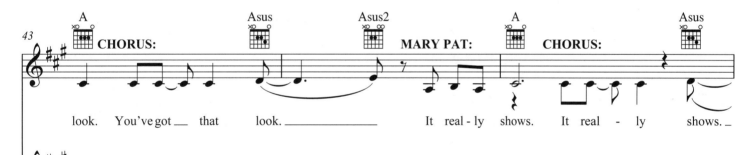

look. You've got _ that look. _____ It real - ly shows. It real - ly shows. _

_____ I can see you walk _ down Ro - de - o Drive, _

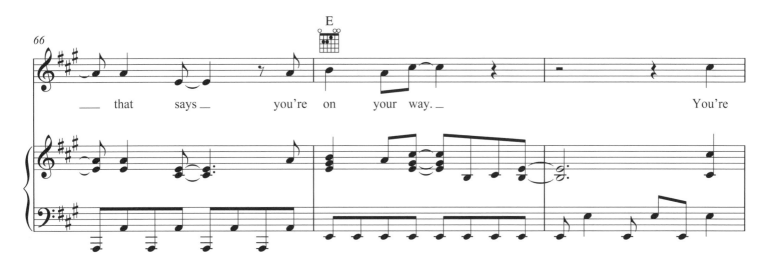

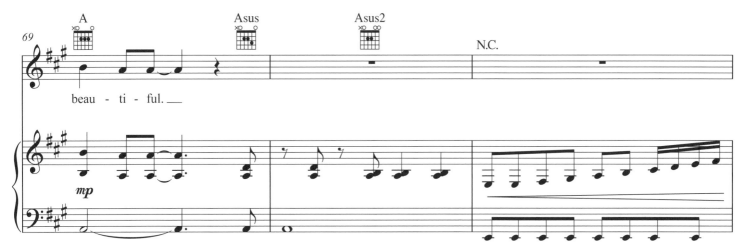

CHORUS: She's got the grace, she's got ___ the groove— I'm start-ing to be-

lieve ___ in her and me.
There's mag-ic in the way ___ she moves— She can take it with ___

___ her wher-ev-er she goes! Where she goes! ___
Where she goes! ___

Where she goes! ___
___ Where she goes! ___

_____ in - side; ___ and for the first time, I _____ can see, ___

- ti - ful! ___ Beau - ti - ful! ___

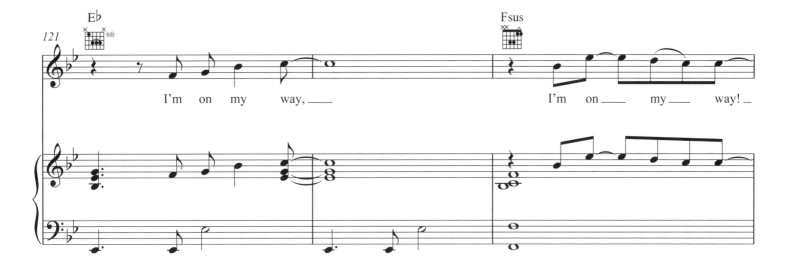

I'm on my way, ___ I'm on ___ my ___ way! ___

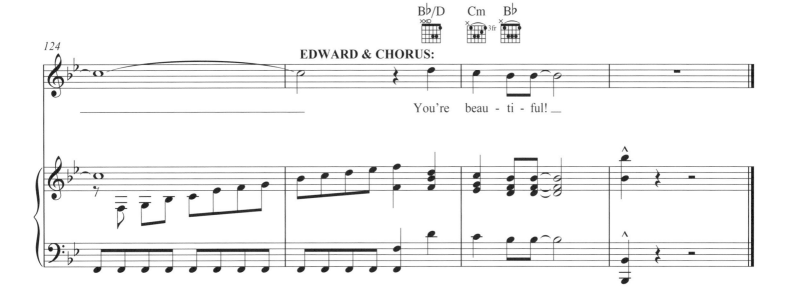

EDWARD & CHORUS:

You're beau - ti - ful! ___

WELCOME TO OUR WORLD
(More Champagne)

Words and Music by BRYAN ADAMS
and JIM VALLANCE

Driving Rock

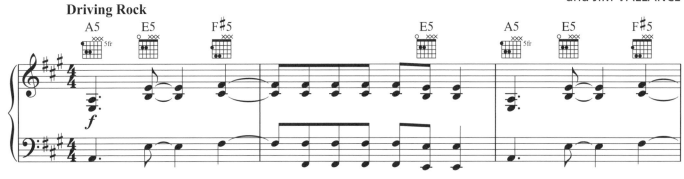

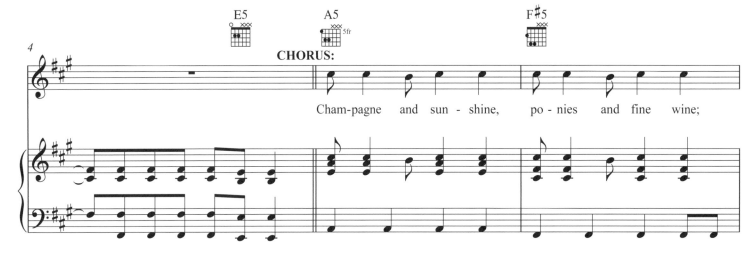

CHORUS:

Cham-pagne and sun - shine, po - nies and fine wine;

who would-n't want to be us? Nev - er a tiz - zy,

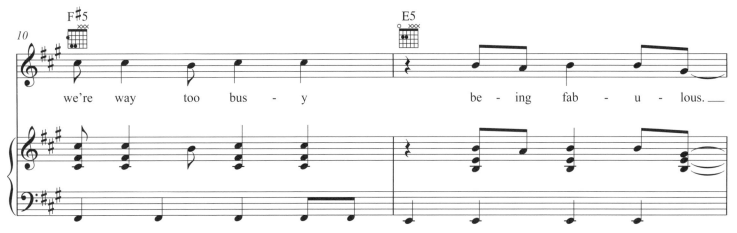

we're way too bus - y be - ing fab - u - lous. __

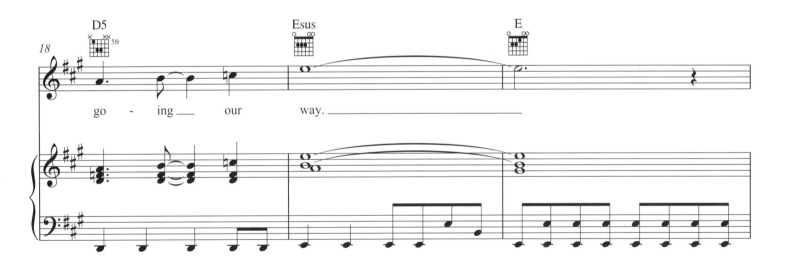

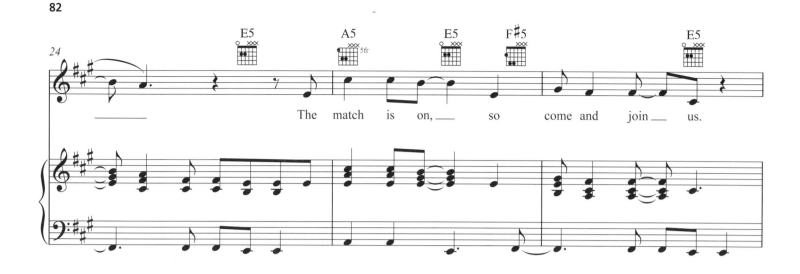

The match is on, __ so come and join __ us.

Wel - come to our world. __ More cham-pagne!

Clink

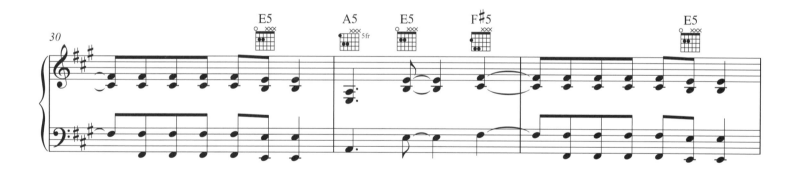

STUCKEY:

Cou - ples or so - lo, we all love po - lo,

the sport of kings and queens. ___ Be - fore we con - tin - ue, we

need your as - sist - ance, and you know what that means. ___

___ It's the age - old ___ tra - di - tion ___ where

we re - po - si - tion ___ the div - ots. ___ Don't

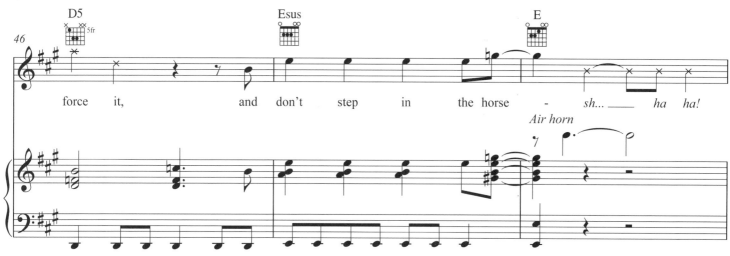

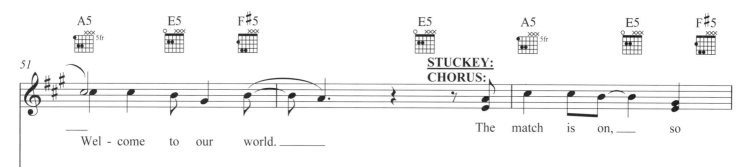

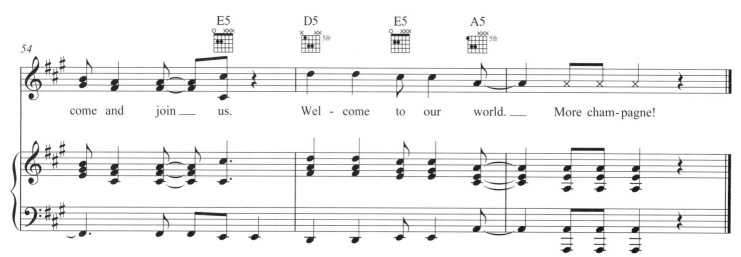

THIS IS MY LIFE

Words and Music by BRYAN ADAMS
and JIM VALLANCE

The first guy __ I loved __ was a los - er; __ the

sec - ond guy was e - ven worse. __ If there was a bum __ with - in

fif - ty miles, I was drawn to him __ like a curse. __

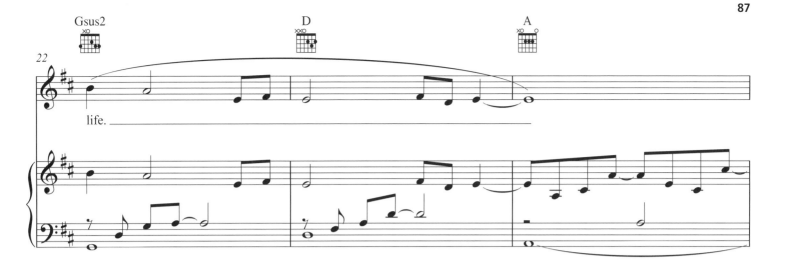

life. _____

I worked at a cou-ple of fast - food joints, __ I parked

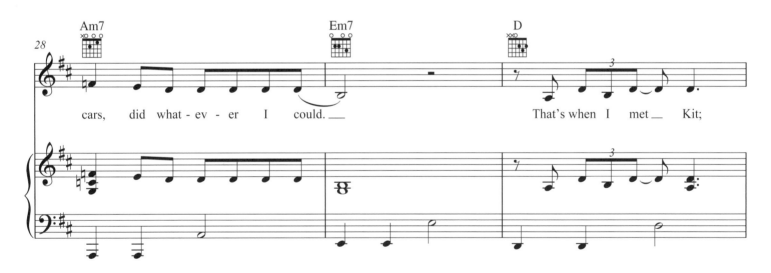

cars, did what-ev - er I could. __ That's when I met __ Kit;

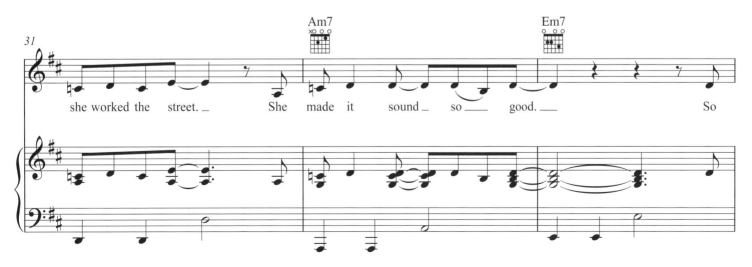

she worked the street. __ She made it sound __ so __ good. __ So

one day, I did it. I cried the whole time. I was com-ing a-part___ at the seams.___

___ It's not like an-y-bod-y plans___ it. No, it

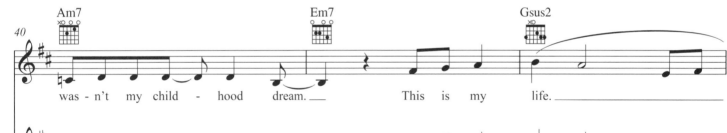

was-n't my child - hood dream.___ This is my life.___

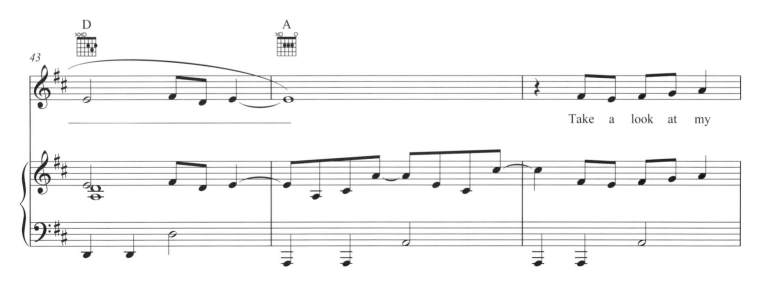

___ Take a look at my

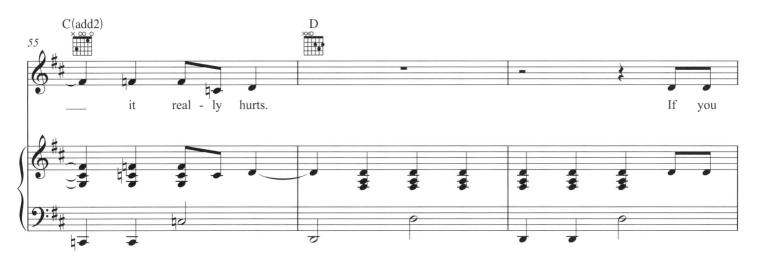

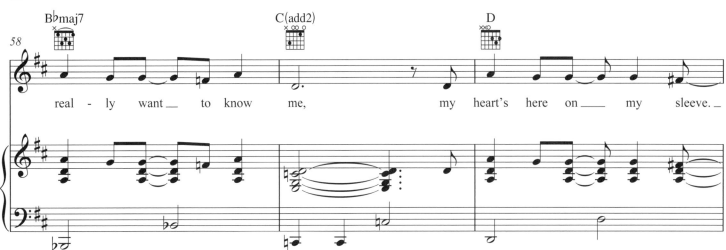

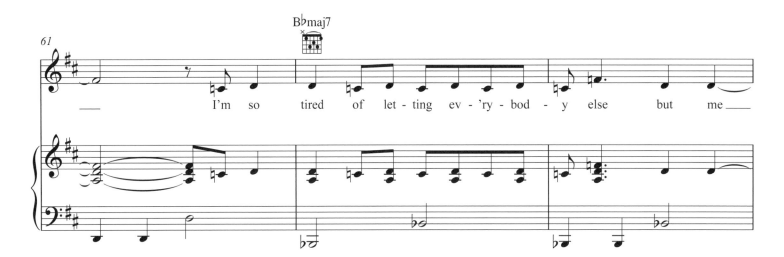

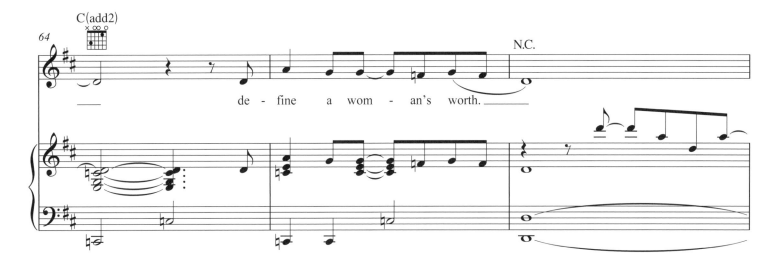

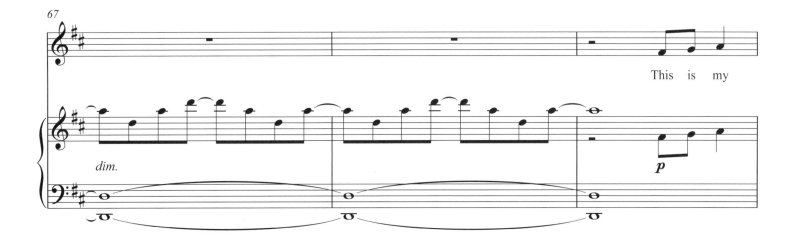

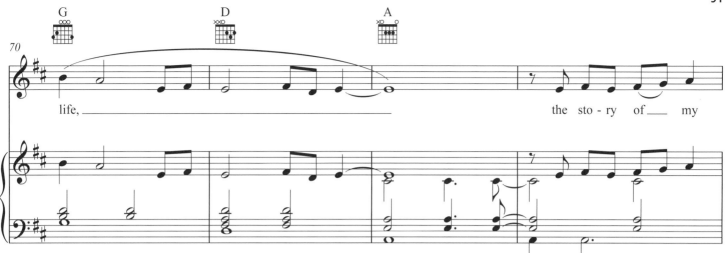

life, _____ the sto - ry of ___ my

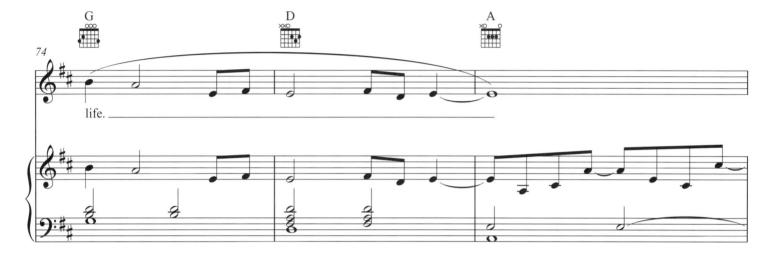

life. _____

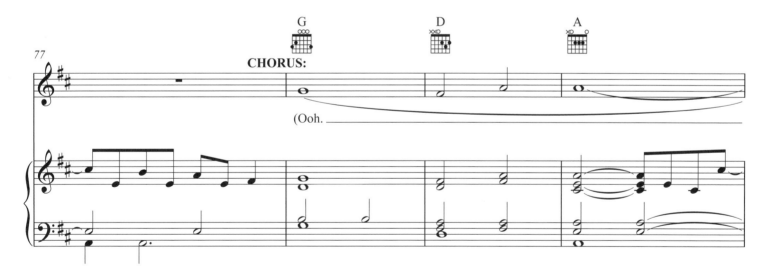

CHORUS:

(Ooh. _____

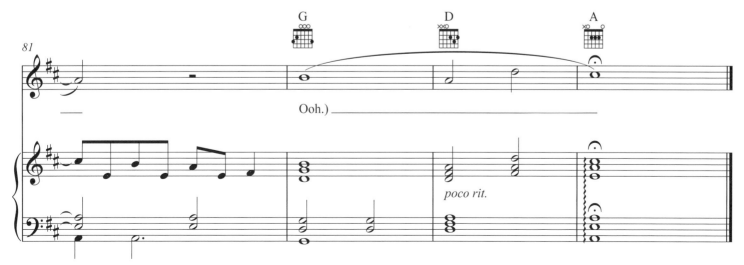

___ Ooh.) _____

poco rit.

NEVER GIVE UP ON A DREAM

Words and Music by BRYAN ADAMS
and JIM VALLANCE

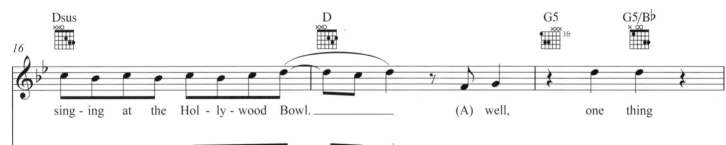

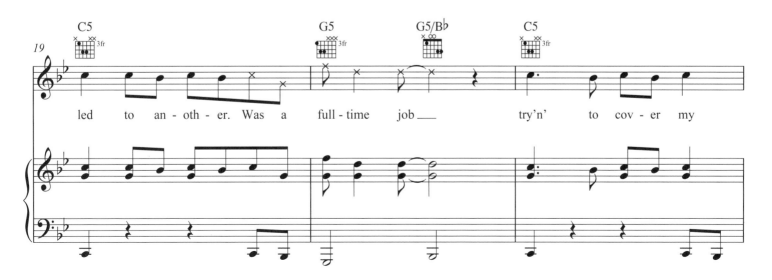

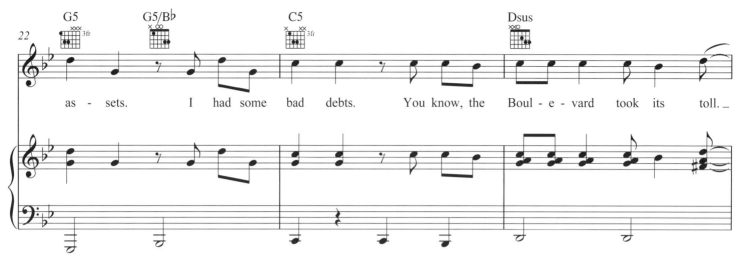

as - sets. I had some bad debts. You know, the Boul - e - vard took its toll. __

_____ But I've still got some fire in my bel - ly. Stand back, and

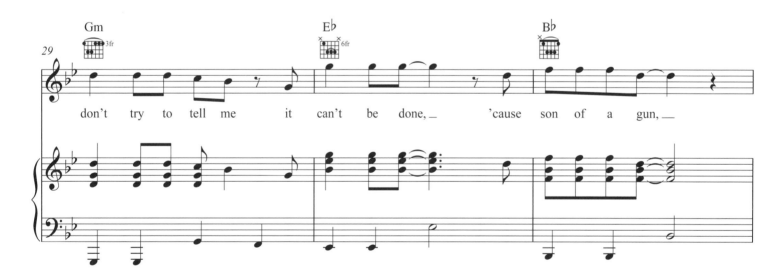

don't try to tell me it can't be done, __ 'cause son of a gun, __

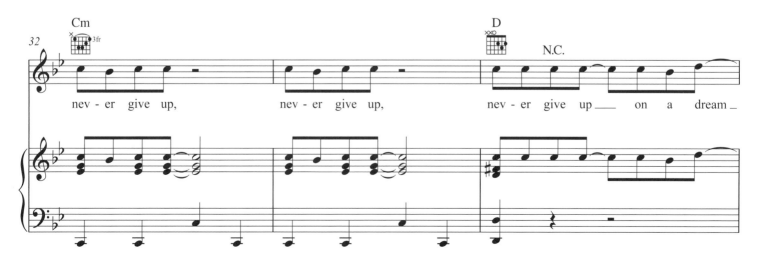

nev - er give up, nev - er give up, nev - er give up __ on a dream __

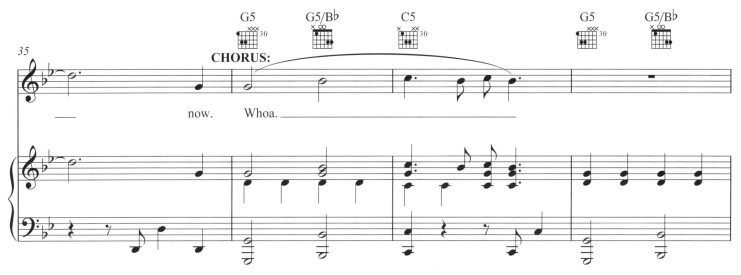

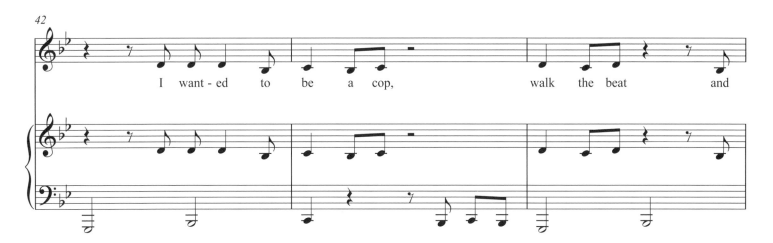

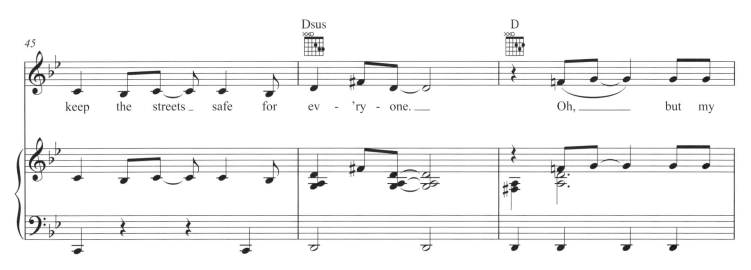

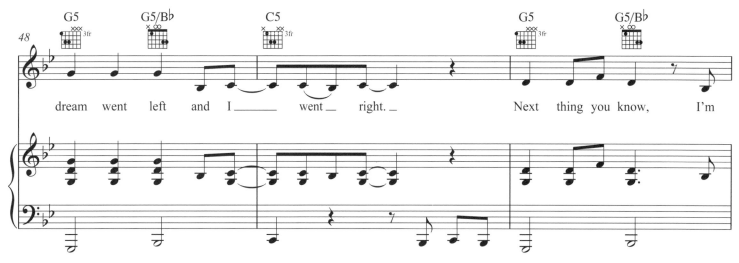

dream went left and I _____ went _ right. _ Next thing you know, I'm

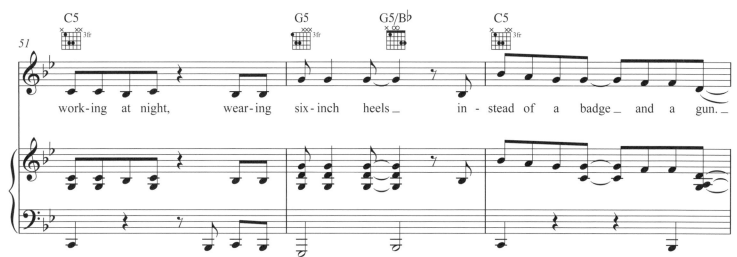

work-ing at night, wear-ing six-inch heels _ in-stead of a badge _ and a gun. _

HAPPY MAN:

_____ Yeah, but you _ still got some cards on the ta-ble.

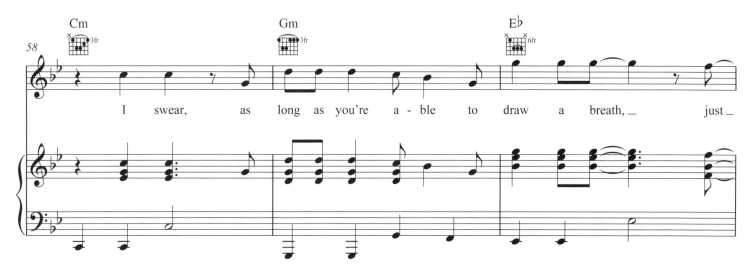

I swear, as long as you're a-ble to draw a breath, _ just _

do your best. ___ Nev - er give up ___ on a dream. ___

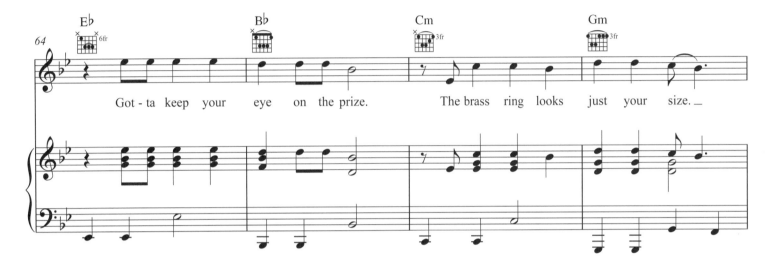

Got - ta keep your eye on the prize. The brass ring looks just your size. ___

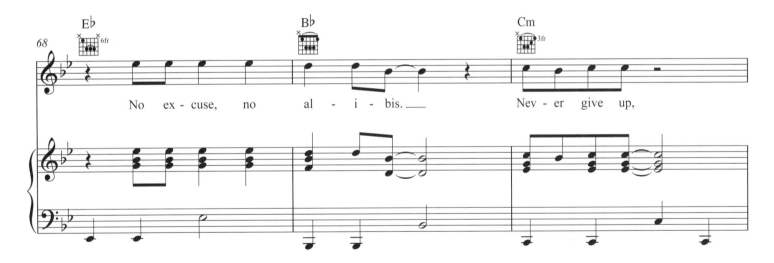

No ex - cuse, no al - i - bis. ___ Nev - er give up,

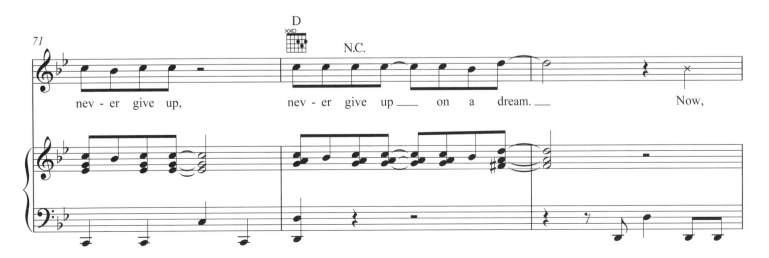

nev - er give up, nev - er give up ___ on a dream. ___ Now,

in - vite the dream; you know what I mean?＿ You got - ta seize the op - por - tu - ni - ty and

go to ex - tremes.＿ Find your dance, now, and take a stance, now, and em -

pow - er the ho - ur of chance, now. So go chase it; don't you waste it. There's a

KIT: **HAPPY MAN:**

pie in the sky;＿ I can al - most taste it. Nev - er give up ＿ on a

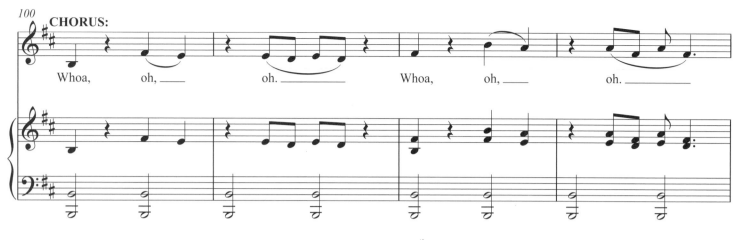

CHORUS:

Whoa, oh, ___ oh. ___ Whoa, oh, ___ oh. ___

C#5

HAPPY MAN (at pitch):

Whoa, oh, ___ oh. ___ Come on! Yeah, yeah! _

F#5 Bsus2 F#5 Bsus2 F#5

add KIT: **KIT:**   N.C.   **CHORUS:**

Yeah! ___ I'm not ___ giv - ing up! (Hey!)

F#5 Bsus2 F#5 Bsus2 F#5   G#5 C#sus2 G#5 C#sus2 G#5

N.C.   N.C.

KIT:
HAPPY MAN (at pitch):   **add CHORUS:**

You're not ___ giv - ing up! We're nev - er ___ giv - ing up!

YOU AND I

Words and Music by BRYAN ADAMS
and JIM VALLANCE

Deep Groove Ballad

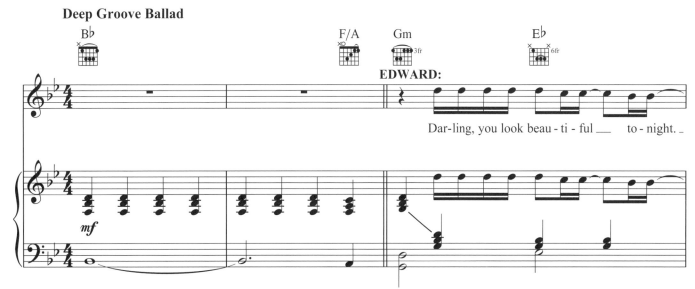

EDWARD:

Dar-ling, you look beau-ti-ful __ to-night. __

I can't re-mem-ber ev-er see-ing an-y-thing __ so right.

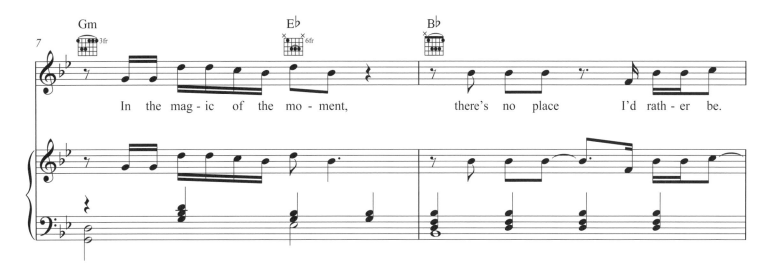

In the mag-ic of the mo-ment, there's no place I'd rath-er be.

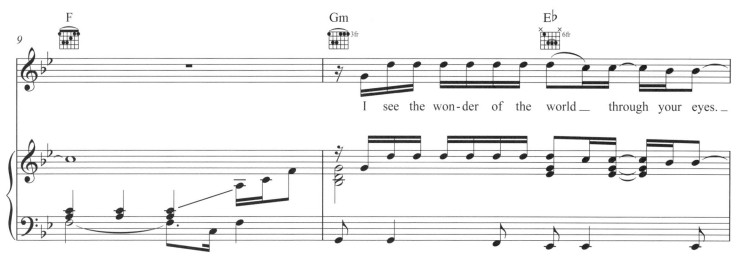

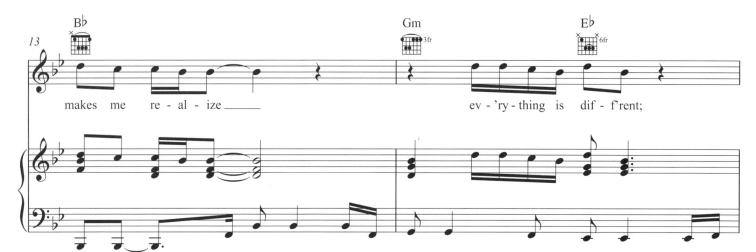

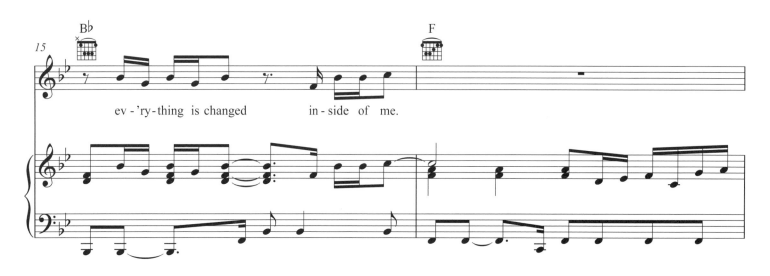

You and I, we got some-thing go - ing on. ___

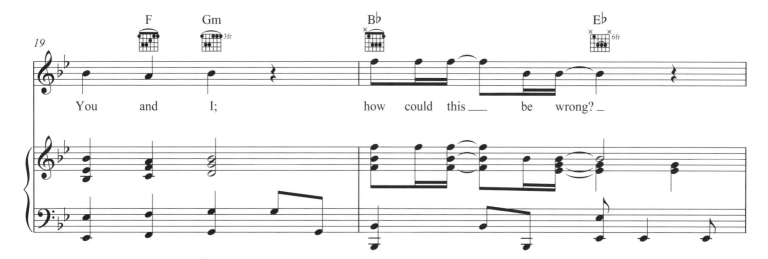

You and I; how could this ___ be wrong? _

Who'd be - lieve _ that we _ could catch the wind ___ be - fore _ it's gone? _

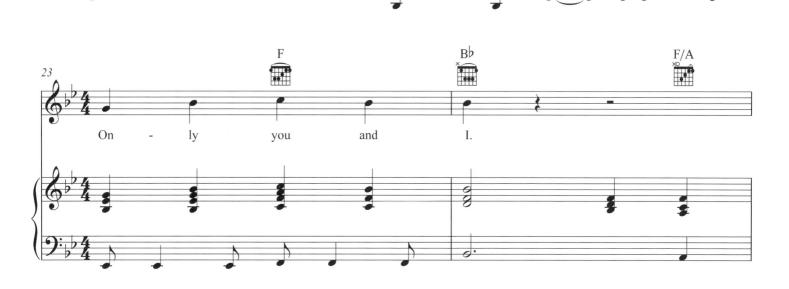

On - ly you and I.

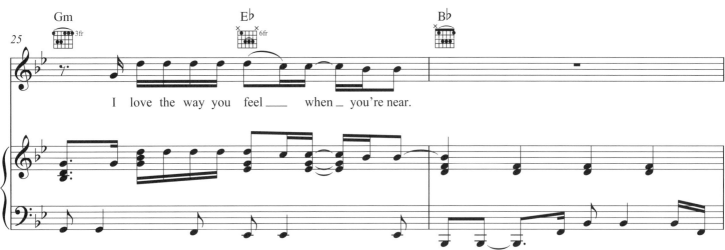

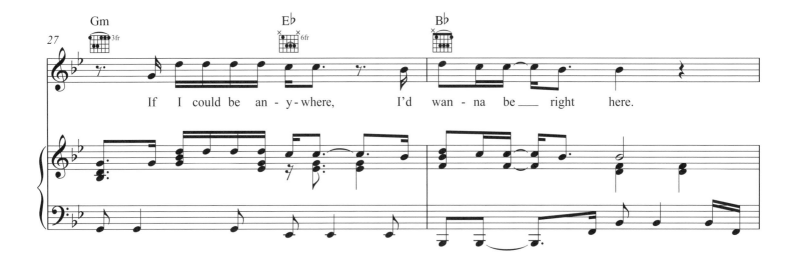

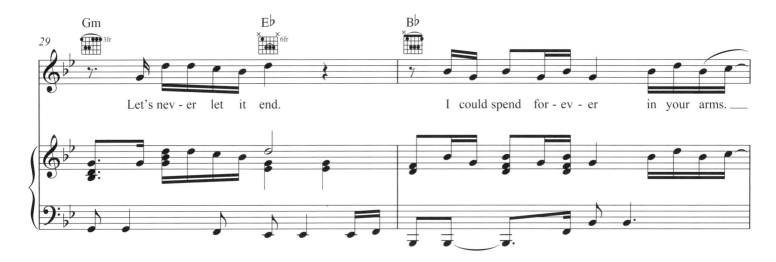

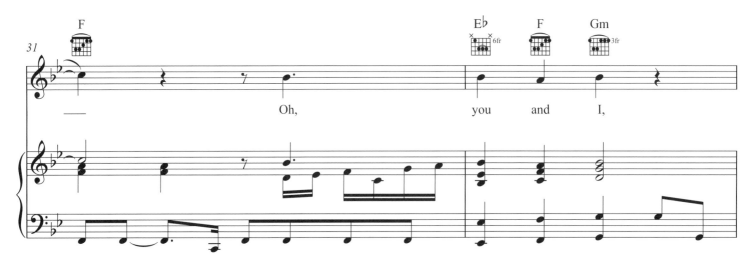

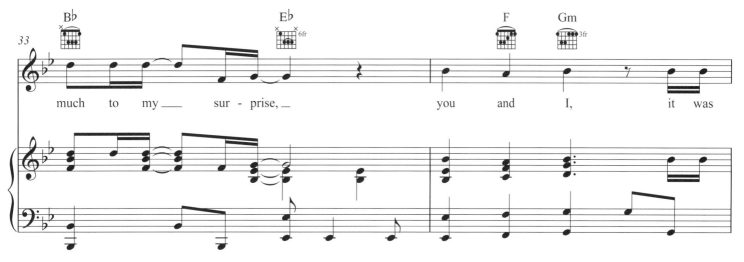

much to my ___ sur - prise, ___ you and I, it was

right be - fore ___ my eyes. ___ I would give ___ al - most an - y - thing: ___ the stars, ___

___ the moon ___ and the sky, ___ all for you and _____

___ I. I was - n't wait - ing for _____ a mir - a - cle; ___

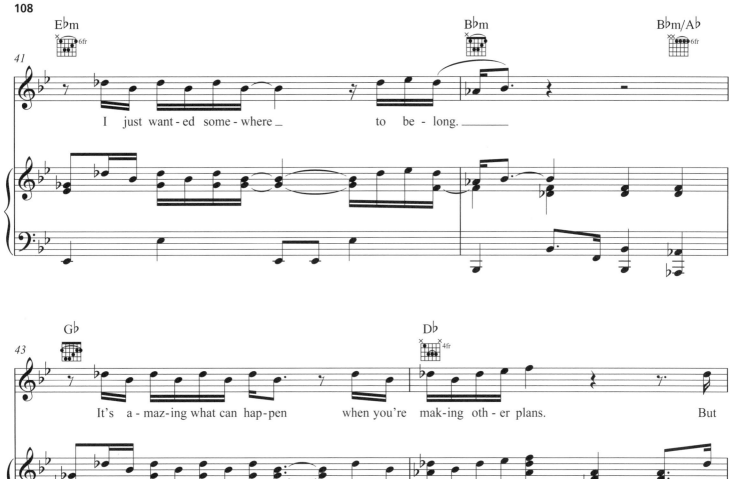

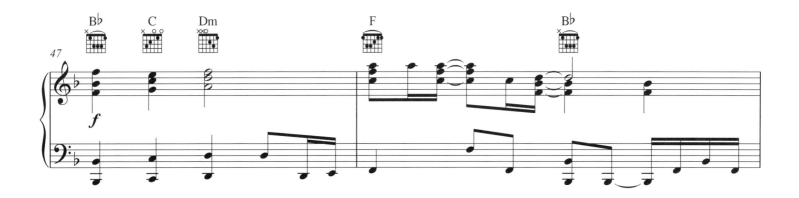

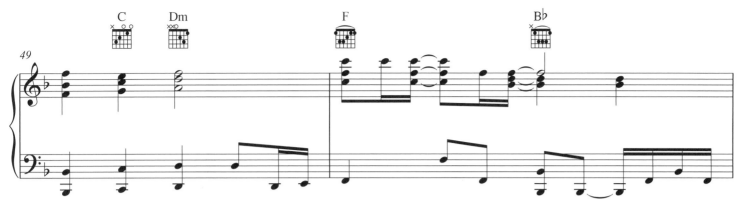

Dar-ling, you look beau - ti - ful ___ to - night. ___

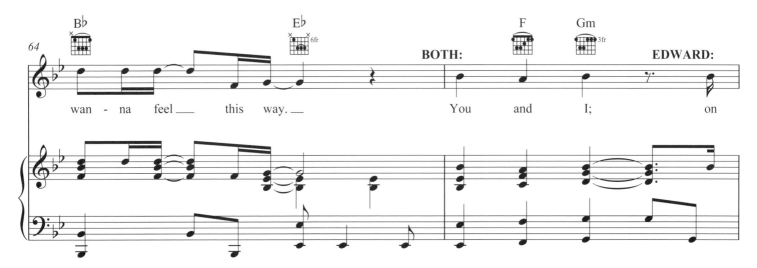

an-y oth-er day,__ I might have missed__ the mo-ment. Now

I just wan-na stay__ to-geth-er, you and

I._____ For-ev-er, you and____

I._____

poco rit.

I CAN'T GO BACK

Words and Music by BRYAN ADAMS
and JIM VALLANCE

You make me hap - py; you know just what to say. ___ But

I ain't Cin - der - el - la. Who'd wan - na be, an - y - way? ___ Of

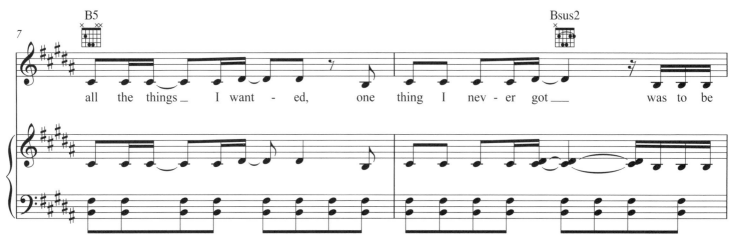

all the things ___ I want - ed, one thing I nev - er got ___ was to be

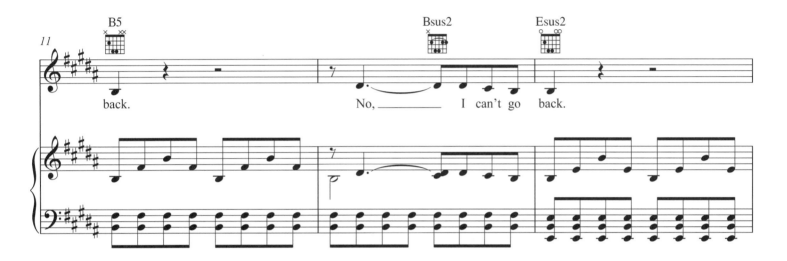

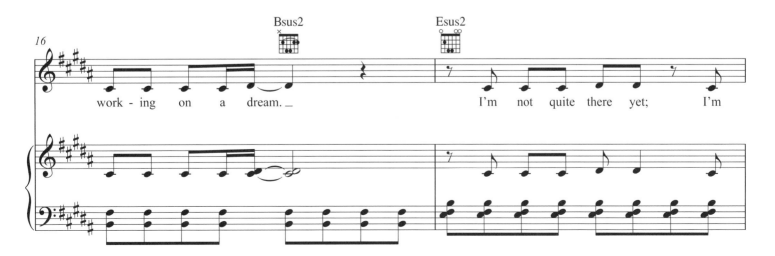

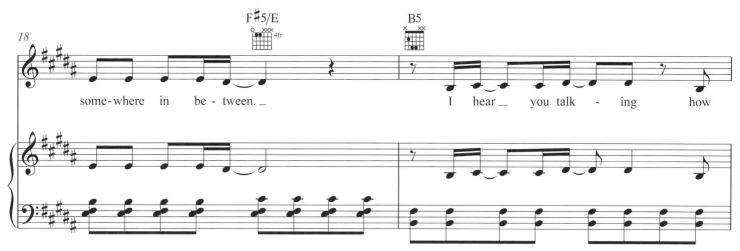

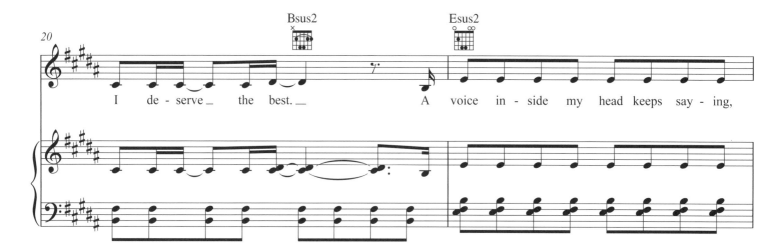

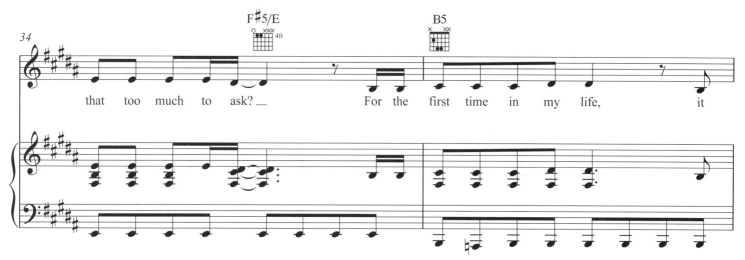

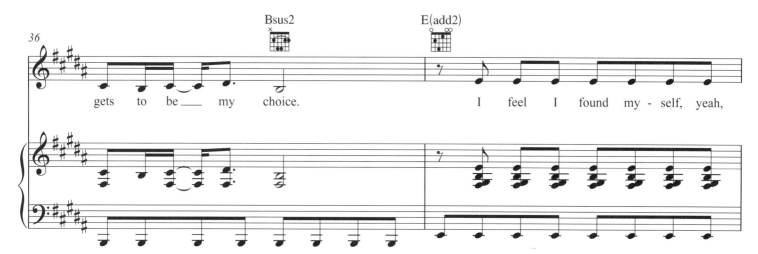

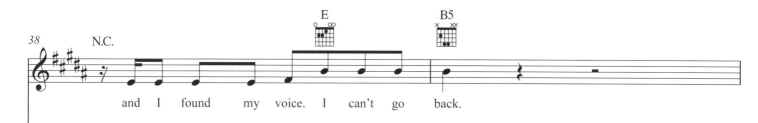

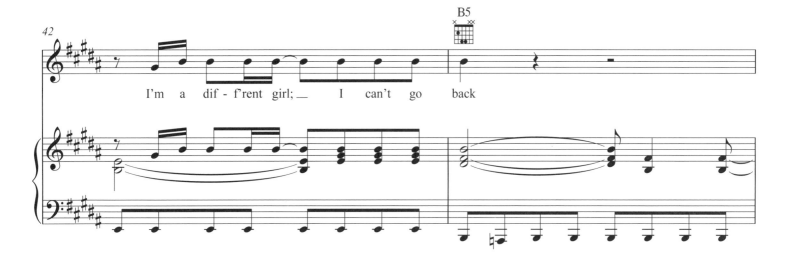

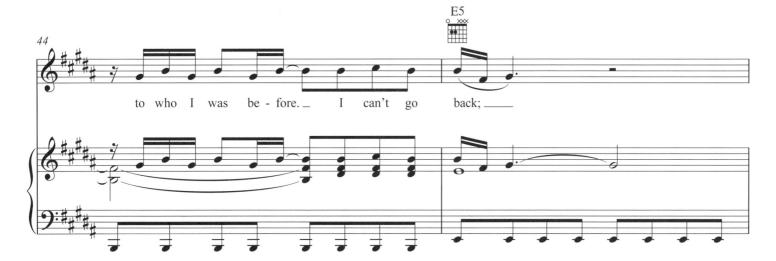

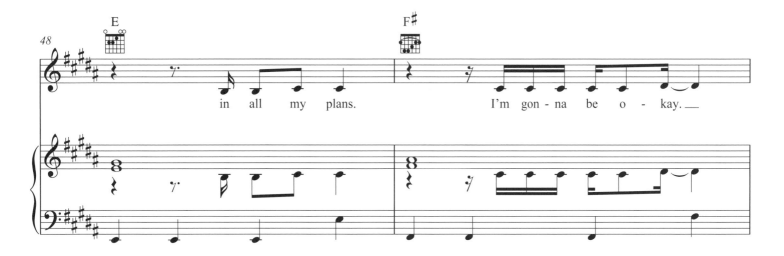

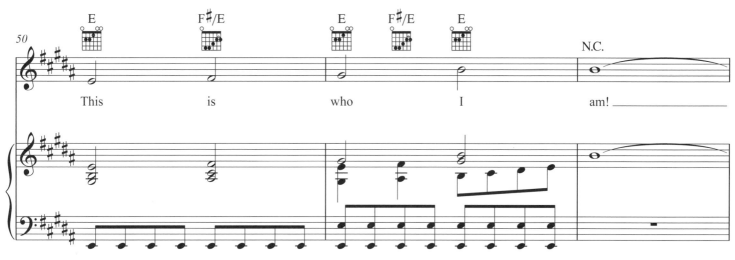

This is who I am! ___

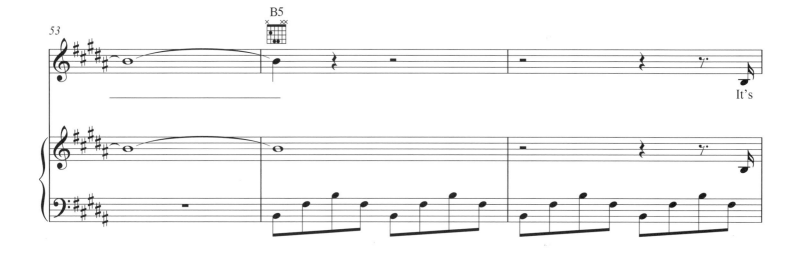

___ It's

true I sold my bod-y, but I nev-er sold my soul. I've

learned I don't need an-y-one; it's me who's in con-trol. ___ They can

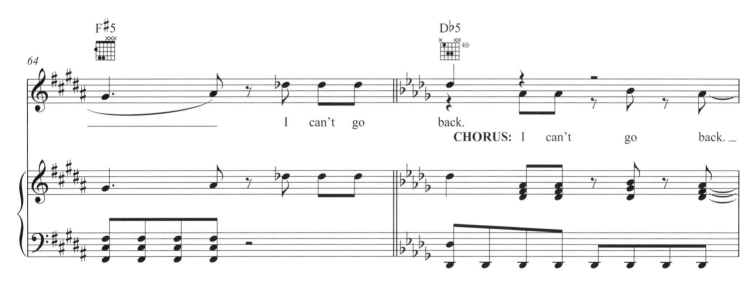

LONG WAY HOME

Words and Music by BRYAN ADAMS
and JIM VALLANCE

used to be, and it's a long _____ way _____ home,

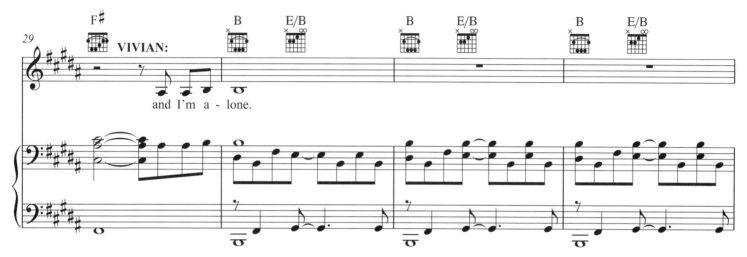

and I'm a - lone.

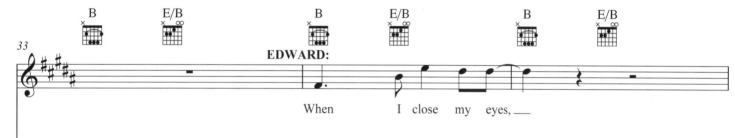

When I close my eyes, ___

when the jour - ney ___ ends, there's a warm em - brace, the fa -

mil - iar face of a _____ friend. 'Cause I be -

VIVIAN:

I be-lieved in you, and you be-lieved in me, long _____ way _____

lieved in you, and you be-lieved in me, and it's a long _____ way _____

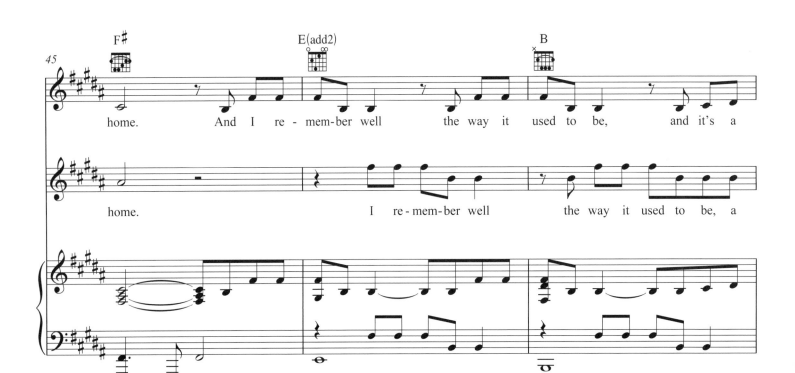

home. And I re-mem-ber well the way it used to be, and it's a

home. I re-mem-ber well the way it used to be, a

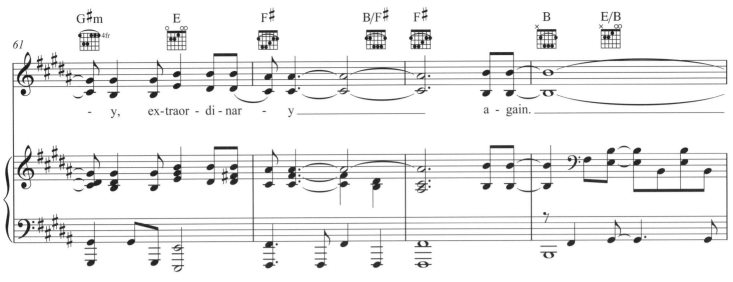

- y, ex-traor - di - nar - y _____ a - gain. _____

_____ 'Cause I be - lieved in you, and you be - lieved in me, and it's a

CHORUS:

I be-lieved in you, and you be-lieved in me,

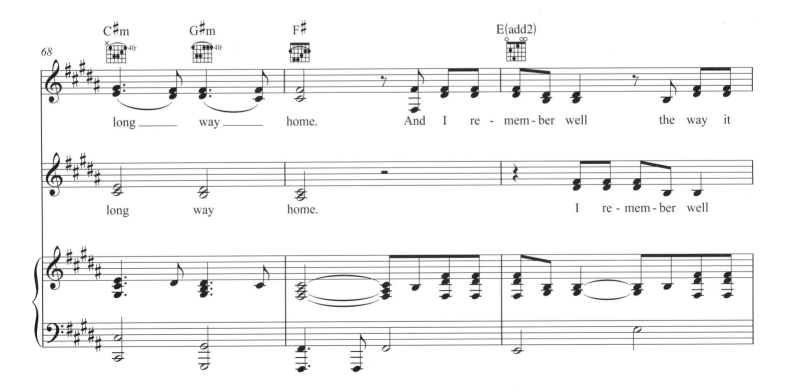

long _____ way _____ home. And I re - mem - ber well the way it

long way home. I re - mem - ber well

used to be, and it's a long _____ way _____ home,

the way it used to be, long way home.

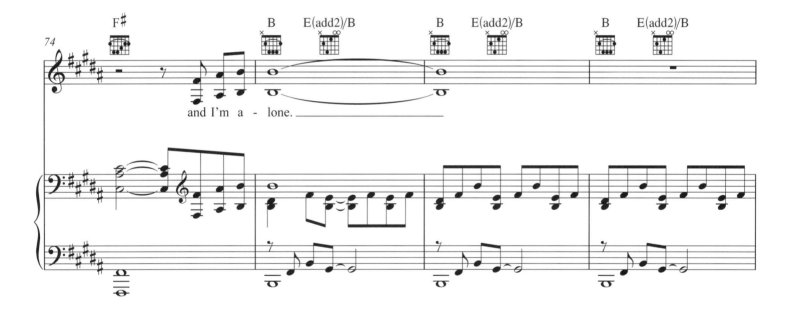

and I'm a - lone. _____

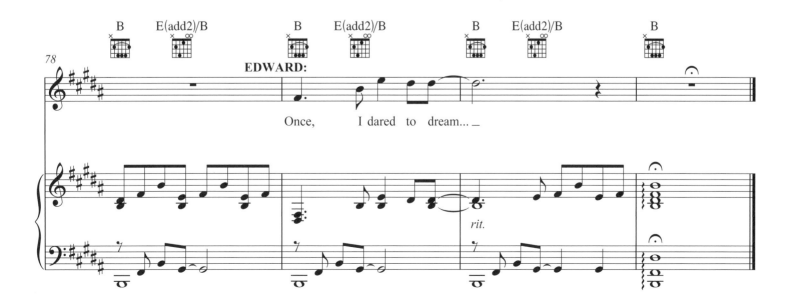

EDWARD:

Once, I dared to dream... _

TOGETHER FOREVER

Words and Music by BRYAN ADAMS
and JIM VALLANCE

Moderate Disco groove

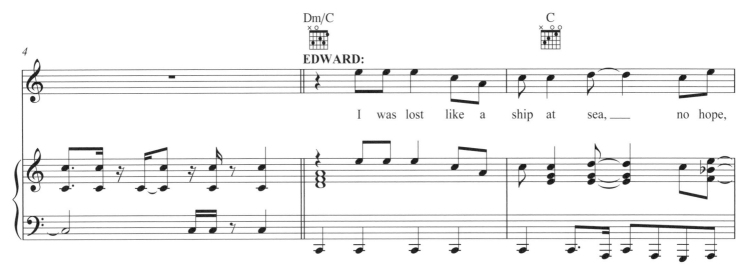

EDWARD:

I was lost like a ship at sea,___ no hope,

no faith, no___ plan.___ You fill my cup, and you

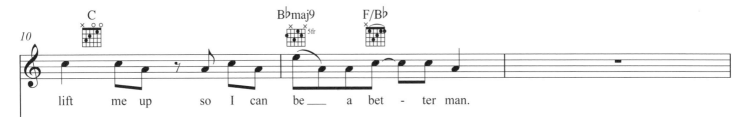

lift me up so I can be___ a bet - ter man.

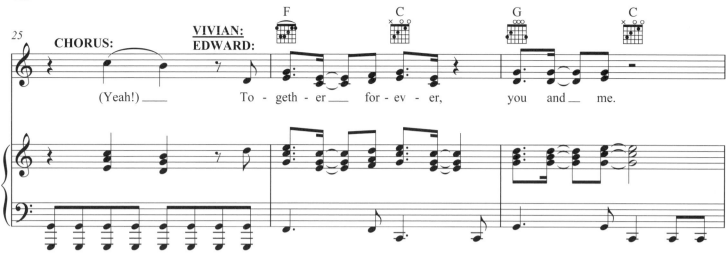

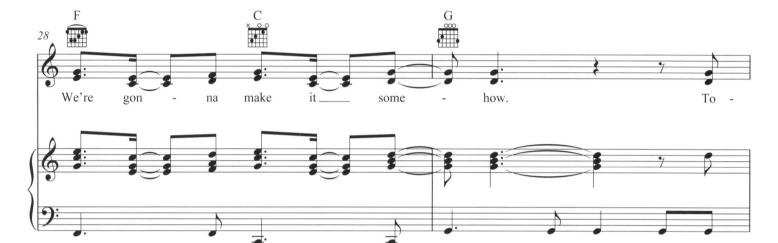

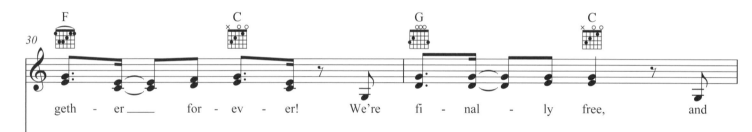

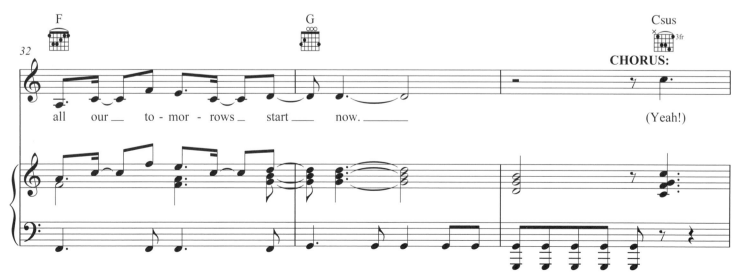

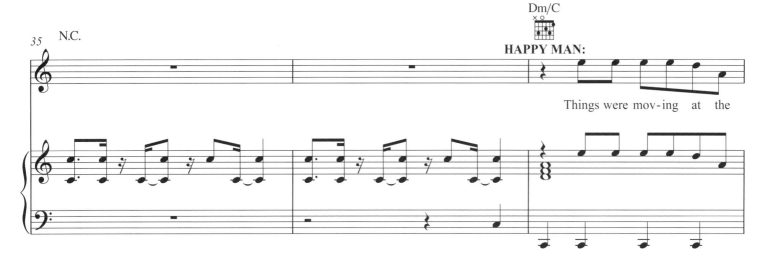

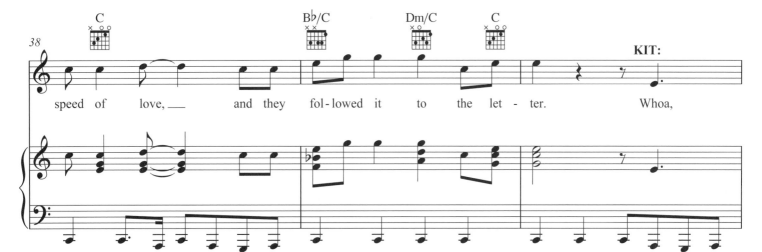

geth - er ___ for - ev - er! We're fi - nal - ly free and all our ___ to - mor - rows ___ start ___

geth - er ___ for - ev - er! Fi - n'lly ___ free!

___ now. ___ Oh, yeah! To - geth - er ___ for - ev - er,

N.C.

you and ___ me. We're gon - na make it ___ some -

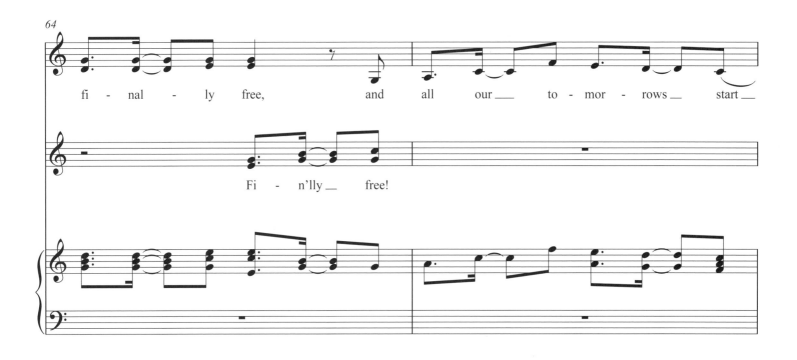

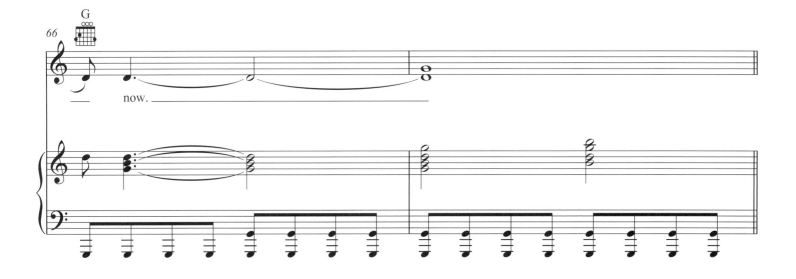

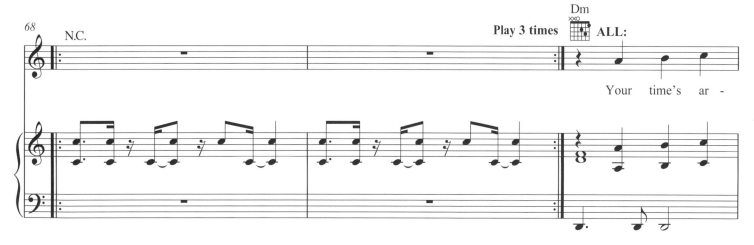

Your time's ar-

rived, you know it. This town's a-live, you own it. To-

geth- er ___ for- ev- er! Wel- come ___ to Hol- ly- wood! ___

MORE OUTSTANDING VOCAL SELECTIONS
from Hal Leonard

00313505	The Addams Family	$17.99
00130669	Aladdin	$19.99
00241528	Amélie	$17.99
00322334	American Idiot	$24.99
00148752	An American in Paris	$17.99
00172978	American Psycho	$19.99
00197874	Anastasia	$19.99
00322401	Anything Goes (2011 Revival Edition)	$17.99
00313285	Avenue Q	$17.99
00276002	The Band's Visit	$19.99
00250379	Be More Chill	$17.99
00123827	Beautiful: The Carole King Musical	$17.99
00312511	Disney's Beauty & The Beast	$22.99
00125618	Big Fish	$19.99
00313432	Billy Elliot	$17.99
00138578	The Bridges of Madison County	$19.99
00175428	Bright Star	$17.99
00119255	Bring It On	$19.99
00251958	A Bronx Tale	$17.99
00313310	Brooklyn The Musical	$14.95
02502276	Caroline, Or Change	$19.99
00119339	Carrie: The Musical	$17.99
00359465	Cats	$19.99
00322415	Catch Me If You Can	$19.99
00117502	Chaplin	$16.99
00251959	Charlie and the Chocolate Factory: The New Musical	$17.99
00312087	Chicago	$16.99
00119879	Rodgers & Hammerstein's Cinderella on Broadway	$17.99
00156632	The Color Purple	$17.99
00313497	Come Fly Away	$19.99
00250241	Come from Away	$19.99
00313384	Curtains	$19.99
00226474	Dear Evan Hansen	$22.99
02501744	Death Takes a Holiday	$19.99
00313305	Dirty Rotten Scoundrels	$19.99
00313490	Dreamgirls – Broadway Revival	$17.99
00313643	End of the Rainbow	$16.99
00155689	Finding Neverland	$19.99
00123635	First Date	$17.99

00277717	Disney's Frozen	$19.99
00125464	A Gentleman's Guide to Love and Murder	$16.99
00313633	Ghost – The Musical	$17.99
00359902	Godspell – Revised Edition	$16.99
00322252	The Golden Apple	$75.00
00313365	Grey Gardens	$17.99
00155921	Hamilton	$22.99
00313219	Hairspray	$19.99
00322290	High Fidelity	$21.99
00194941	Holiday Inn – The New Irving Berlin Musical	$17.99
00146103	Honeymoon in Vegas	$16.99
00234732	The Hunchback of Notre Dame	$19.99
00313411	In the Heights	$19.99
00153584	It Shoulda Been You	$17.99
00119278	Jekyll & Hyde	$17.99
00313335	Jersey Boys	$17.99
00123602	Jesus Christ Superstar – Revised Edition	$17.99
00251079	John & Jen	$17.99
00124376	A Night with Janis Joplin	$16.99
00360286	Les Misérables – Updated Edition	$19.99
00313466	Legally Blonde	$17.99
00313307	The Light in the Piazza	$19.99
00259008	The Lightning Thief	$17.99
00313402	The Little Mermaid	$22.99
00313390	A Little Princess	$19.99
00313303	Mary Poppins	$17.99
14042140	Matilda – The Musical	$19.99
00313503	Memphis	$17.99
00313481	Merrily We Roll Along	$17.99
00313535	Million Dollar Quartet	$16.99
00121881	Motown: The Musical	$16.99
14048350	Natasha, Pierre & The Great Comet of 1812	$19.99
00322265	Next to Normal	$22.99
00103051	Nice Work If You Can Get It	$16.99
02501411	Nine	$19.99
00313498	9 to 5	$19.99
00122181	Now. Here. This.	$16.99
00313617	The People in the Picture	$16.99
00450151	Peter Pan	$14.99

00360830	The Phantom of the Opera	$19.99
00313376	The Pirate Queen	$17.95
00313591	Priscilla, Queen of the Desert	$16.99
00313525	Rain: A Tribute to the Beatles on Broadway	$19.99
00313069	Rent	$22.99
00313460	Rock of Ages	$19.99
00126814	Rocky	$16.99
14042919	The Rocky Horror Show – 40th Anniversary Book	$19.99
00158983	School of Rock: The Musical	$19.99
00322322	See What I Wanna See	$16.99
00151276	Something Rotten!	$19.99
00313518	The Sound of Music	$22.99
00313302	Monty Python's Spamalot	$19.99
00313644	Spider-Man: Turn Off the Dark	$17.99
00313379	Spring Awakening	$22.99
00322460	The Story of My Life	$24.99
00322245	Striking 12	$16.95
00190369	The Theory of Relativity	$17.99
00313435	13: The Musical	$19.99
00313455	[title of show]	$16.99
00190505	Tuck Everlasting	$17.99
00321950	The 25th Annual Putnam County Spelling Bee	$19.99
00130743	Violet	$16.99
00204751	Waitress	$17.99
00249705	War Paint	$17.99
00450165	West Side Story	$24.99
00313268	Wicked	$19.99
00322260	The Wild Party	$19.95
00313298	The Woman in White	$17.99
00313613	Women on the Verge of a Nervous Breakdown	$17.99
00313404	Young Frankenstein	$22.99

www.halleonard.com

Prices, contents, and availability subject to change without notice.